Against All Odds

ELLIE GOLDSTEIN

Against
All
Odds

THE *UNSEEN*

First published in Great Britain in 2023

Society for Promoting Christian Knowledge
The Record Hall, 16–16A Baldwins Gardens
London EC1N 7RJ
www.spck.org.uk

British Library Cataloguing-in-Publication Data
A catalogue record for this book is available from the British Library

Hardback ISBN 978–0–281–08821–8
eBook ISBN 978–0–281–08822–5
audio ISBN 978–0–281–08823–2

1 3 5 7 9 10 8 6 4 2

Typeset by Fakenham Prepress Solutions
First printed in Great Britain by Clays Limited
Subsequently digitally printed in Great Britain

eBook by Fakenham Prepress Solutions

Produced on paper from sustainable forests

Contents

Contents

Foreword

It's safe to say that to know Ellie Goldstein is to love her.

Ever since I first saw her in the Gucci Beauty advert that took the world by storm in 2020, I was drawn to her cheeky smile and undeniable charm. We all needed a piece of Ellie's effervescent joy – especially during that pandemic year. And I'm delighted to say that nothing about Ellie is an act; she exudes the same genuine happiness and confidence in real life, too. As soon as Ellie walks into a room, you know about it.

One of my favourite memories of Ellie – of which there have been many – was when we came together to shoot the publicity images for The UnSeen. Within moments of her being there, the most serious team members were singing along to Ellie's favourite tunes ('Islands in the Stream' by Dolly Parton and Kenny Rogers was the song of the day) and twerking along with her! Ellie's joy is so infectious that you can't help but get swept up in it – something I'm sure you'll see just a few short pages into her story.

But of course, there is a significance to Ellie's life that underscores all of the wonderful silliness she invites us into. Even during my first glimpse of her in that Gucci Beauty campaign, I felt a reverence for what those images signified. I was so happy to see representation within high-end brands and the beauty industry; something I have been painfully aware was lacking ever since my own life-changing event that marked me forever and made me feel truly UnSeen.

The impact of Ellie's presence and personality on the modelling industry and beyond cannot be underestimated. It is an impact that becomes all the more special once you understand the odds stacked against her. Ellie's tenacity and ability to prove every naysayer in her life wrong is truly inspirational. Hers is the kind of story which shows us that even when it feels as if the mountains we need to climb are insurmountable, there is nothing we can't face with a willing spirit and a grateful outlook – provided we take it one step at a time.

As you'll read in the pages of this fantastic book, Ellie hasn't had the easiest of lives. It has been full of uncertainty for her and her family, and to make matters infinitely harder, wider society hasn't always been kind about her disability, making Ellie feel 'othered' and 'unseen' among some of the circles in which she has found herself. Even so, Ellie has continued to be a trailblazer. In the absence of anyone like her to follow, she has created her own normal. I felt a similar isolation after the event that changed my life and, with no one to look up to, I went out and created my own path, living with a visible difference.

Of course, few of us become trailblazers alone. We have families and support systems that hold us up when times are hard. For me, this is one of the most touching aspects of Ellie's book. The relationship between Ellie and her mum reminds me of parts of my journey with my own mother. I love what they stand for as a family; never giving up or giving in to stereotypes. She has really raised Ellie to believe that she can do anything, and it's true.

Reading about how Ellie has defied the odds and continues to go from strength to strength in her life and career cannot fail to leave a lasting impression on you. Not only will Ellie's story help you to seize life and practise gratitude, but I truly believe it will encourage you to have a deeper understanding of others. You may not have a disability yourself or be in close contact with someone who does, but that doesn't mean you cannot become an ally of those affected by disability. We all have a responsibility to make society a more accepting place for us all to live in.

I am so proud that Ellie's book is the first in my new The UnSeen imprint. The more stories like this that are heard, the more it will break down the taboo of visible difference in society. There is so much unfounded fear surrounding some people with disabilities, which of course only creates more division and dehumanises people. Books like this help us to educate ourselves, remove fear and see the person behind the disability. If Ellie can take on the odds and prosper, why can't we also play a small part in making the world a safer, kinder and more accepting place for all people? I believe it is a cause worth fighting for… against all odds.

Katie Piper OBE

Introduction

The first thing you should know about me is that I am happy. Before writing this book, I sat down with my mum Yvonne and looked over my life so far and, even though I knew that at times I was supposed to feel down or upset, I just didn't. The world, to me, is an exciting place. I get to dance and laugh my way through it, surrounded by people I love. And I hope that, no matter who you are and why you decided to pick it up, my story will leave you feeling a little happier, more confident, and free to be whoever you were made to be.

From my very first memory, my life has been filled with joy. Though it's hard to say which precise memory came first (you try writing an autobiography – it's hard to remember everything!), I'm pretty sure it's from when I went horse riding as a child. This wasn't galloping through the fields with my hair blowing in the wind like on TV, though – before you get any ideas. I always wore a helmet and usually had a kind attendant at the end of a lead, helping me to trot around. But I loved every second of it.

I rode two horses: Tansy and Swampy. Don't ask me what size they were; all I knew at the time was, compared to six-year-old me, they were *massive*. Then again, I'm still only four foot nine (1.4m), so if I met them today I would probably still think they were big! Two horses clearly weren't enough for little me, as, in addition to the open-to-all riding school I was attending, I was also on the waiting list for a special needs one. That's because I was born with Down syndrome, so I needed different care from a lot of other people – especially when I was younger.

The thing was, I was quite good at horse riding (and it's not just me who would say that – ask my mum).[1] I loved to stroke the

---

1   Yvonne: Yeah, to be fair, she was pretty good at horse riding!

horses' necks and bounce around as I was led through the park. But when I got to the special needs riding school, they had a different plan for me. I still loved the ponies and riding around, but they didn't try to teach me any new tricks or push me to progress. Instead, we walked around in a circle with the horse for half an hour and then it was time to go home. I already knew that I could do so much more.

Have you ever felt like people underestimate you? Or just look at you and assume they know what you are capable of? That's how I felt. And sadly, it wouldn't be the first or the last time that someone put me in a 'Down syndrome box'. Walking around in circles was definitely safer than the riding I was doing at my first school, but if there's one person who has always known that I was better than the box people put me in, it was my mum – and she promptly pulled me out of that class. I wanted to be out of my comfort zone, and she was happy to help me get there as long as I agreed to take it one step at a time. We all need a champion, don't we? Well, as you'll see, she's always been mine.

Mum knew that I was capable of so much more than those people assumed. There was a big wide world of horse riding, exercising and dancing out there, and I was missing it because I was just walking around in circles. You see, I'm not bothered by the challenges I face. I like to push myself and have others push me, too. I know I can do a lot, and I love having the opportunity to show people – especially the ones who doubt me. And, as you'll see throughout the pages of my book, a lot of people have doubted me along the way.

As with any life, there have been highs and lows, and I hope in reading them that you, too, will discover that no one has the right to put you in a box. You weren't made to go round and round in circles, either. I surprised the riding school with what I was capable of, and I've surprised lots of other people, too. But to give you the whole story of my life, we can't start here. My horse riding at six years old isn't the real beginning. It all started with my mum and the biggest surprise *she* got in her life: me.

1
A change of plan

Yvonne's story

My life changed when I became a mother – how could it not? As those of you who have been fortunate enough to have children know, nothing is ever the same again. I had my first daughter Amy when I was thirty years old. She was bright but reserved. She never tried to be the centre of attention, and she always seemed older than her years. She was affectionate, and even at a young age we could see that she was kind. My husband Mark and I were besotted. You never realise the impact a child will have on your life until you hold your own in your arms. Nothing could have prepared me for Amy, and I never would have believed that I had so much love to give.

We knew we didn't want Amy to be an only child, and she definitely didn't want that either. As she saw her friends getting younger brothers and sisters, she started asking us for a sibling. We dreamed of that picture-perfect family with two sweet children and a cat or two. I would have loved a boy, of course, but I secretly hoped for another girl. She would be the ideal companion for Amy, and they could play together and get up to mischief.

We started trying for a second child, but things didn't go smoothly. Over the following years I had four miscarriages; each one more heartbreaking than the last. My body didn't seem to care where I was or what I was doing, and I was always out of the house when I realised I was miscarrying. Once I was on an aeroplane and another time at a Chinese restaurant. I felt the familiar stomach cramps and knew it was happening again. Each time we would go to hospital to be told we had lost our baby. After the fourth time I decided it just wasn't going to happen.

We worked hard to make sure that Amy didn't feel like an only child. We constantly had her friends over to stay – she had a busier social life than either of us! But we hadn't given up on the idea of growing our family, so we made the decision to adopt.

Anyone who has tried to adopt a child will tell you that the process is long. It can feel never-ending. After eighteen months of forms and meetings, including interviews between our case worker and Amy, we were finally approved. By this time I was thirty-eight, and we were excited to start talking about who this little person – the one who would complete our family – might be. We told the adoption team that we would like to welcome an older child, rather than a baby. But they explained that any child we adopted would need to be younger than Amy, so it was likely that we would be given a baby. Just as the wheels were finally set in motion, I realised my period was late.

I couldn't explain what it was – it wasn't morning sickness or tiredness or anything like that – but all of a sudden I felt different. I told Mark, and we agreed that I should take a pregnancy test. I brought the test back to the house and did it in the bathroom. I couldn't believe it when I saw the second line pop up on the small panel. We were pregnant again! Little did we know then of the worry and wonder that would come in welcoming our Ellie into the world.

I told Mark, and he was so happy. We were nervous and didn't want to get ahead of ourselves after previous disappointments, but we couldn't believe we might be having a second child of our own. The only catch was, we would have to inform the council and we would no longer be eligible to adopt.

The adoption team was happy for us, but it was made clear that we couldn't continue as planned. That was just the rule. This made the pregnancy bittersweet. We were over the moon to have our own baby, but we'd also set our hearts on adoption. Our mindset and focus had been on how to welcome someone else's biological baby into our family and show them all the love we possibly could. We had been through a lot to get to that point, and we hadn't made the decision lightly. With hindsight I can see I felt guilty that I would no longer be offering someone else a home. I felt like, after all the work we had put into the process, we were letting a lovely little child down. But it just wasn't meant to be.

My pregnancy went well. I was lucky both times round not to suffer from any extreme morning sickness. I went off tea and coffee during both pregnancies, and suddenly the smell of orange and lemon was disgusting to me, but other than those very minor things it was an easy ride.

I told Amy virtually straight away. She was only seven years old, but she was switched on and mature for her age. She understood that something was up before we even had the conversation. I remember her excitement at the news, and the day she gathered all her friends to tell them she was to have a brother or sister. None of her friends' parents had such a big gap between their first and second, but I didn't mind so much. I was just excited about doing it all over again.

I have an unusual blood type, so the doctors were sure to run additional tests on me and the baby to make sure we were both doing well. I wasn't alarmed by this, as it had been the same procedure as when I was pregnant with Amy. Everything was normal. Every scan came back fine. My gynaecologist screened for Down syndrome and the results indicated that I was in a very low-risk category. I asked if they intended to follow up with an amniocentesis – the test that checks for birth defects such as Down syndrome in the baby. But as we were low risk, I was told there was no need.

At the twenty-week scan, Mark found out the baby's sex but I didn't want to know. The scans weren't so accurate those days, so you couldn't be 100 per cent sure, but he wanted to prepare himself and I wanted the surprise. I was so excited to welcome a gorgeous new addition to our family that I didn't care if it was a boy or a girl, as long as it was healthy and happy. And with the pregnancy going so smoothly and all the test results looking great, I began to relax and believe that things were looking up. I started to think our challenges were over and we could just focus on our blessings.

The official due date was 25 December 2001 – Christmas Day! But in the run-up the baby moved around, so it wasn't in a safe position for delivery. Rather than risk a natural birth, the hospital scheduled a Caesarean section for 18 December. I didn't want a C-section; I'd had a natural birth with Amy, and I wanted the same again with this second child. I didn't like the idea of a long recovery period, especially as I had a seven-year-old daughter who would also need my time and attention. But it wasn't my choice, and I had to do what they advised was best for the two of us.

Early on the morning of 18 December, Mark and I went into hospital. We took my cream duffle bag, stuffed full of things for me and the new baby. My mum stayed home with Amy, and I couldn't wait to walk back through that door a day or two later to rest in my own bed with my new baby by my side.

We got to the hospital at 7 a.m., but there was a bit of a wait before we were seen. By the time they'd run all the tests and had us prepped for theatre it was 1 p.m. Mark came into the operating room with me. He was wearing all the gear you see on TV: the face mask, hat and gown. They put a screen between my head and my stomach, so I couldn't see what was happening. But Mark has never been squeamish, so he was peering over the panel, keen to catch the first glimpse of our new arrival.

I had an epidural, so was completely numb from the waist down. It wasn't painful, but I could feel a bizarre pulling from my stomach as they removed the baby. I remember feeling anxious. I was desperate for it all to be over so we could go home.

At 1.31 p.m. they removed the tiny baby from my stomach and rushed her to one side. I caught a look at the side of her little body as they whisked her away – she was completely purple. The cord had been wrapped around her neck and she hadn't been able to breathe. I couldn't hear anything. No cries, no murmurs, nothing.

They swiftly unwrapped the cord from around her neck and did something to clear her airways. I couldn't work out what they were doing, and they were too focused to tell me. I felt helpless. And then I heard a cry. I was so relieved! Surely that was good. Surely it meant I had a healthy baby. But still no one said anything to us. I asked if everything was OK and got no response.

After what felt like a lifetime they put her on the scales, noted down her weight of six pounds and five ounces, and brought her over to me. The team was still sewing up my stomach when I got my first proper look at our gorgeous baby girl. They didn't let me hold her, but Mark stole a quick cuddle. I could tell something was wrong. Even though no one explained what was happening, there was a tension in the room. I asked yet again what was going on. And that's when the midwife said: 'We think she's got Down syndrome.'

2
What *is* Down syndrome?

A word from Ellie

I just wanted to jump back in to say that I've never felt different for a single day, but I know that in some ways I am. Down syndrome is a disability, but I'll never let it stop me.

If you're not sure what Down syndrome is (or want a reminder), here's some science stuff. A person is born with Down syndrome; you can't catch it. It's nothing to do with anything either parent did before or during the pregnancy. It just happens by chance. A baby who is born with Down syndrome has one extra chromosome. Chromosomes, which hold the DNA that make us who we are, are usually arranged in pairs, but I have one set of three.

You think it's pretty rare, don't you? Well, it's not as rare as most people assume. One in every thousand babies in the UK is born with Down syndrome. Fifty per cent of those babies are born with a congenital heart defect, which makes it five times more likely that they won't live past the first year of their life.

Actually, while we're talking about it, disabilities in children in general aren't as rare as people think. The charity Growing Hope (www.growinghope.org.uk), which provides free therapy for children with additional needs, was set up by Naomi Graham. She told me that 17 per cent of children in the UK education system have additional needs. That's like a sixth of every school! Not everyone's needs are the same as mine, though. Some can be physical or learning-related, or to do with their mental health.

Naomi explained that sometimes additional needs, like Down syndrome, are diagnosed at birth or even before birth, but other times the parents just start to realise that their baby isn't developing as predicted – maybe they're not crawling or walking or talking or making friends as expected.

Everyone who has Down syndrome is different and, as with all people, they have their own personalities (as you'll see, mine's pretty cheeky), things they like (dancing, for me) and things they don't like (peanut butter on toast – yuck!). Some people can live independently and have a job, while others need more care and support. I'm somewhere in between. I have a job (the best job in the world), but I also have care from my mum and family to make sure I'm always looked after and OK.

There's a lot more information online, and plenty of stories from people with Down syndrome and their families. I think the NHS website (www.nhs.uk/conditions/downs-syndrome) and Down's Syndrome Association (www.downs-syndrome.org.uk) are pretty helpful if you'd like to know more.

All right, back to Mum's part of the story...

3
Meet Ellie

Yvonne again

The medical staff took Ellie away again almost immediately. Mark and I were stunned. We just looked at each other; neither of us said anything. I felt exhausted and confused, and I couldn't process what the nurse had just told us. Everything around us felt rushed and frantic, but we were just still, unsure of what to do or say next.

They took us out of theatre and put us straight into a private room. At any other time I would have considered a private room in an NHS hospital a luxury, but I knew that we had been separated from the other patients because something was really wrong.

I have no idea how much time passed before they wheeled in my little girl. She had a plastic tag around her delicate wrist and her face had that crumpled look of a newborn who would really rather have stayed in the warmth of its mum's tummy. But still no one was talking to us. We were told to wait in the room and that the doctor was coming. You know that dread you feel when something's going to happen, but you don't know what it is or how bad it's going to be? That's how it felt. And as any of you who have felt it know, it's *excruciating*.

They wouldn't let me feed her. Every time I got someone's attention to ask if I could try her with a bottle, they told me no. They said she might have problems feeding, so we just had to wait. She screamed and screamed, desperate for something to eat, but we were still told to just wait. I didn't even pick her up; I didn't know what to do. I felt so weak and confused. Mark held her and tried to soothe her, but I knew she just needed some milk. My head felt so hazy.

I looked at my husband and asked, 'What did that woman say?' We didn't think it could be right. Not after the test had come back clear. We were low risk; the doctor had said it. Mark said he didn't know what she was talking about. We looked into the little plastic cot and examined her face. We couldn't see anything abnormal. To me she looked like her sister Amy, although she had less hair. Amy was born with a mop of dark locks, but Ellie had less. I thought she was cute, but I wanted to know what they were seeing that made them think something was wrong.

My mum and Amy had come to the hospital to see me and meet the baby after the procedure, but they weren't allowed into the room. The hospital staff refused to let any visitors in to see us.

We were left waiting for the doctor for hours. I kept asking when someone was coming, but I was never given a straight answer. I felt annoyed and worried and tired and muddled all at once, but the worst was that unsettling feeling I mentioned before.

After a four-hour wait, the doctor walked in. He didn't come alone; there were another seven people with him – other doctors and nurses from the ward. They marched into the room like an intimidating army of white coats and blue pinafores. No one sat down, no one greeted us. No one even gave us a smile.

The lead doctor walked over to Ellie and picked her up from the cot. Her dinky frame could hardly hold on to the little nappy they had put on her. He lifted her up to shoulder height, holding her with one hand, his elbow bent and her tiny body just slumped next to him like a piece of meat. He said, 'This is Ellie. She's got Down syndrome. She won't walk, she won't talk and she won't go to university.'

I gaped at him. I didn't know what to say or how to react. It felt like my brain was processing everything in slow motion, but the situation was moving so quickly.

My husband said, 'What do we do, then?'

The doctor explained there was a stand outside with leaflets that should give us some more information. Leaflets? Lifeless, faceless, *leaflets*? We didn't ask any other questions. We didn't know what to say, what to ask or where to start.

I told the doctor I needed to feed her, and he said he didn't know if she would be able to feed. He said she probably had jaundice and then reeled off a list of other complications they said she could have. It seemed as if he was expecting everything to go wrong with her; like he had already written her off on the first day of her life. I couldn't believe what was happening.

He left the room, and one by one the entourage filling the space around us filed out behind him. A kind nurse lingered behind to apologise on his behalf for 'the way it was handled'. Then she slipped out, leaving me, Mark, Ellie and one other nurse in the room. I asked for a bottle so I could try to soothe my distressed baby.

The nurse turned to us and said, 'Last month we had one of these babies and the mum left it here. What do you want to do? Do you want to do that?'

It was the final slap in the face. I looked at Mark and he looked back at me. I don't think we even answered her.

When we were alone, I finally fed my little girl. She latched on to the bottle with no problem. Even then, drinking for the first time, she clamped the teat with her gums when I tried to take the bottle out of her mouth and she wouldn't let go. Her small features even started shaking with the pressure. I have no idea how she knew to do that. She was just desperately hungry. She was less than a day old, but as her jaw gripped the bottle there was so much fight in her. I watched her feed and wondered how they could be right. How could she grow to be so incapable when she was already so determined?

The nurse came running in to see if she had fed OK and asked if she had been sick. I told her no, everything was fine. That was the first time Ellie proved the people who doubted her wrong. It would be the first of many. Even then she was a force to be reckoned with.

The following day the hospital sent in a counsellor to speak to Mark and me about having a baby with Down syndrome. The woman walked into the room where we were waiting and stood there, arms crossed, simply staring at Ellie. By this time, I was coming out of my haze and I felt angry. Really angry. Justifiably angry. I asked her if she had anything to say or if she had just come to have a look. When it became clear that she wasn't going to be of any help, I asked her to leave and told her not to come back. By then I felt sure that the hospital wasn't going to be the place where I would get my support.

In the years that followed, we had loads of doctors' appointments and met with many amazing medical professionals. I am so grateful for the treatment and kindness they have shown Ellie over the years, but on the day she was born they let us down. Missing a diagnosis or misdiagnosing a condition can happen. Doctors are only human, after all, and often they are rushed off their feet. But it's painful and hard to process when it happens.

Norah Myers, who works as a disabled Pilates instructor, was diagnosed with cerebral palsy at birth. She was thirty-six when she got a second diagnosis of multiple sclerosis, but at first it was misdiagnosed as transverse myelitis. She told me how confused and frustrated it had left her. Getting her correct diagnosis gave her a sense of calm as it meant she knew how to move forwards, but after being in the dark for a while, she felt really low. Thankfully she's been able to let go of her anger, and I think that's where I'm at now, too. But it took a long time.

Two days after the C-section was the last day of the winter term for Amy's primary school, and she was starring in the Christmas play. Poor Mark went to watch our eldest girl sing and dance around the stage with all of this going on in his mind. I doubt he remembers a single thing about the show. I imagine he thought his head was about to explode.

Neither of us had a clue what to expect from a child with Down syndrome. All we knew was what we'd seen on telly, or when we'd occasionally walked past someone on the street who looked visibly different in the same ways we had seen in the media. Lots of people still assume that Ellie will be exactly like someone else they've met with Down's, but even then she was so unique. Rex Brinkworth, who founded the Down's Syndrome Association in the 1960s, was told that his beautiful daughter Francoise would just be a 'vegetable' because of her Down's diagnosis, but he said he wouldn't let the 'severe under-expectation, and... conventionally negative medical prognosis' stop him and his wife from doing all they could for their little girl.[1] It's sad that so much time had passed, yet I still experienced something similar with Ellie.

In years gone by, Ellie would have been put in an institution with other 'mentally ill' people. Much like the nurse who suggested I abandon her at the hospital, parents were encouraged to leave their kids in these institutions and never look back. The children were badly treated and were refused any education or healthcare. I can't even imagine how awful that must have been; not only for the children themselves, but for their entire families.

Growing Hope's Naomi Graham says that she thinks people's reactions to those who are 'different' come down to fear, and I completely agree. They don't know what to expect, so they avoid engaging with them at all. Even now, although Ellie is clearly a very capable woman, people look over her head and ask me questions about her. They assume she can't speak for herself, when anyone who has met her properly knows that she is more than capable of speaking! Naomi shared with me that, through the work of her charity and other organisations that seek to support those with additional needs, she hopes that one day everyone will be 'seen and valued for who we are, with our differences, whether they are big or small'. She adds: 'We may feel like these differences define us and make us who we are, but, irrespective of this, I believe there is always hope that we can be valued in our families, friendship groups and wider communities, for the unique and wonderful person that we are.'

I'm so grateful that Mark and I had each other to lean on in those early days. Even though we never really sat down to discuss Ellie's condition, we were able to be each other's rock. I remember him saying at the time, 'We've got a long road ahead. Let's take it step by step.' Sometimes we'll still say that to each other when we have a problem with Ellie's school or we don't know what's going to happen next. It's the approach that's worked best for us.

---

1   C. Boys, '50 Years of the Down's Syndrome Association: So where did it all begin?': https://www.downs-syndrome.org.uk/about-dsa/our-history (accessed 27 April 2023).

Coming to terms with a diagnosis is hard, especially when it's a shock. It can feel like every plan and dream you had for your baby is just falling away in front of you. There's a grieving process you have to go through as you let go of what you thought you wanted and feel the loss of that change.

Back then I wasn't able to think straight, let alone challenge what was happening around me. Now when I look back, the most shocking thing is that no one stopped to comfort me or offer me any encouragement. No one said, 'You can do this,' or 'You're capable of being amazing parents to this little girl,' or 'No matter what the future holds, your baby will thrive in her own way with your love and care.' I wish we'd been told what an amazing life could be waiting for us; that while it would look different from what we imagined, it would hold its own achievements, excitement and a huge amount of joy.

4
What next?

We had to stay in hospital for a while. I had always wondered how parents of multiple children coped when something went wrong and they needed to stay in hospital, or when their child needed some special attention. I soon found out. We were lucky that Mark and I were both around to manage sitting with Ellie and looking after Amy. My mum was also just around the corner, and she helped out a lot. Anyone who has to navigate a difficult and scary time like that without family support or as a single parent has my deepest respect. It's harder than I ever could have known.

In the confusion and shock of finding out about Ellie, I felt like I was in a daze. I was still exhausted and recovering from the operation, and also trying to process what life would be like now. No one really helped us. All we knew was that the doctors expected her to have a low quality of life. I didn't want that for her, but I didn't think there was anything we could do to fight the rising odds against us. Have you ever felt the same way?

Those first weeks in the hospital passed by in a blur. I was so grateful to have Mark there, and we just dealt with each day at a time, without thinking too far into the future. We couldn't do anything else; everything was so unknown. It was terrifying. We didn't even know if Ellie would make it out of the hospital, let alone what sort of life she would have when she did.

The doctors assumed that the Down syndrome meant Ellie would have many other health complications. They spent the week after her birth telling me they were just waiting for the jaundice to kick in, but it never did. As they ran tests, it became clear that Ellie was healthier than they had first thought. Every one of these tests came back negative. This was the second time she had proven those

16

who assumed the worst of her wrong – but there was a lot more of that to come.

There was only one problem that came up and, upsettingly for us, it was a big one. Ellie had a congenital heart defect that meant she required open heart surgery. I already felt like my heart was breaking, but this caused another crack to emerge. She was too small and fragile to have the operation straight away, so we had to wait until she was six months old. I dreaded it. I just wanted the hard stuff to be over. Even when they sent us home with newborn baby Ellie I couldn't relax, knowing we would soon be back there to face another terrible ordeal.

It took time for me to come to terms with everything that had happened during those weeks in hospital. For months I couldn't say it out loud. I didn't say anything to my family. Those words they'd used to describe her – the way the doctors had dismissed her and told me all the things she would never do – I couldn't bring myself to repeat them, even to my mum. When I finally did say something to my close friends, all I could muster was, 'She's got it.' I let them work out what it was she had through a series of yes and no questions, as if we were playing a game and they had to guess the celebrity I was thinking of. Beyond that, I didn't feel I could speak about it – even though, looking back now, speaking up about what I was going through was probably one of the most powerful things I could have done. At the time, the sheer weight of our reality prevented me from opening up in this way.

My mum worked out what was going on, and I confirmed it for her. That's when the family found out. My mum was my rock. She had always championed and supported me, and when my children came along she did the same for them. I can still remember her response. She told me Ellie was perfect. She said there was absolutely nothing wrong with her. Even as Ellie grew up, and I would get fed up or moan at her when she did something wrong, my mum would tell me to leave her alone. In her eyes, Ellie was just as she was supposed to be; an adorable little girl. I was so encouraged when I heard her say that. From words of condemnation to words of affirmation, what we speak over ourselves and to others really, truly matters.

On the whole, everyone's response was very kind. They were concerned for me and for Ellie, and for our family, but I felt supported. One friend did claim that they 'already knew' before I told them, but I tried not to let the occasional insensitive comment bother me.

The person I worried most about telling was Amy. How do you get a seven-year-old to fully understand what it means that her sister has Down syndrome? How would she feel when she found out her new play partner would probably never walk or talk? How much should I tell her? And how much should I hold back until she was a bit older? How could I reassure her that everything would be all right when even I didn't know if that were true?

It took me and Mark months to work out what to say to her and how to say it. In the end, I finally told her that Ellie had a 'condition'. I explained that Ellie wasn't ill, but that her condition meant she would learn things more slowly than Amy had. I can't remember the exact words we used, but I remember how I felt when she burst into tears. I felt guilty.

I wanted to protect both my children. I wanted Amy to know that I would always have enough time and love to give her. I wanted her to feel excited about her sister – not worried or scared. I wanted to be able to protect Ellie from a cruel world that might see her as different. I wanted her to have every opportunity to live life to the full. I wanted her to laugh and get the job she wanted and fall in love. I felt so helpless for both of them.

I reassured Amy as much as I could. She had already come across a young girl with Down syndrome at an after-school club. The girl was adopted and Amy hadn't got on with her. The girl had scared her a little, and on one occasion Amy came home saying that the girl had pulled her hair. Amy assumed that Ellie would be the same. It was hard to comfort her, because none of us knew what to expect. As with any child, we didn't yet know who this little bundle of life and limbs would become. Yet, with Ellie's diagnosis and our lack of education and support around it, the unknowns felt even less quantifiable.

Part of the reason I didn't want to tell people was that I was worried about what they would say. I had a health visitor's appointment a week or so after we got back from the hospital. I had wrapped Ellie up and put her in the pram for a quick walk around, and when I got back the health visitor was waiting by the door. She looked shocked when she saw us approaching and said, 'Oh, you actually took her out, did you?'

I don't know what she meant, and maybe they were just careless words, but I felt judged; as if she thought my baby should be hidden away; as if Ellie shouldn't be seen out in public. It hurt. I started to look at Ellie and wonder what everyone else saw. Did she look like a sweet baby to them, or did other people see something else? Something that shouldn't be taken out of the house?

Every parent thinks their baby is beautiful but wonders how much of that is bias and how much is true, don't they? But I was starting to get really anxious about it. I would stare at her, looking at her alert eyes, darting around and taking in the new world around her. To me she looked cute. She had a little tuft of hair sticking up from her head that reminded me of the Grinch! I just wanted to protect her from other people's harsh looks and judgements, but I couldn't shake the feeling that it would be a long road ahead. And in many ways I was right.

5
Broken-hearted

We got through the first six months of Ellie's life in a bit of a daze. We took it one day at a time, as Mark had said. I loved her, of course I did, but I was still trying to process the shock of what had happened and the terrifying prospect of what might happen next. I found it harder to bond with her than I had with Amy. The awful truth was, I didn't want to bond with her because I didn't know what was going to happen with her heart. I didn't know how long we would have her.

It was hard, knowing that there was a huge – and incredibly dangerous – operation hanging over our heads. The doctors said they wanted to wait until she had gained weight and strength before they did the open-heart surgery. She was a dinky six pounds and five ounces when she was born, and no matter what I did, I couldn't get her to put on weight. It didn't matter how much milk she had, she just wouldn't grow. We went for regular check-ups where they evaluated my tiny, fragile girl, and weighed up when might be the right time to risk dangerous surgery.

The heart condition made her breathing erratic and irregular. Any mum will know the pain of seeing their helpless little child struggling. It felt unfair. I was so desperate for her to just be OK, for the operation to be over and for us to get on with living our lives. We had to take it one day at a time, otherwise we would have gone mad with worry.

The night before the operation, Great Ormond Street Hospital called us in to run through what would happen the following day. They showed us the ward where they would keep Ellie after the surgery, and showed us the tubes and machinery that would be connected to her tiny body. They hoped the preparation time would mean we weren't as shocked when we saw our little girl with hundreds of monitors and wires hooked up to her fragile frame.

The nurse who was giving us the tour ran through what would happen during the operation. All we knew was that it was open-heart surgery to address the holes in her heart, something that affects half of babies with Down's. That was terrifying enough for us, but as the nurse ran through the list of problems they planned to fix, the blood drained from my body. Ellie also had valves missing that they needed to rebuild; something we'd never been told before. It was then that we also found out Ellie would be having bypass surgery. That means they would remove her heart from her body and stop her lungs while a machine made sure the blood continued to pump around her body.

I stood there, listening to all this new and alarming information. My mind was whirring, trying to process one terrifying sentence after another. The nurse had been reading from our file, so she must have assumed we had already been told all this. I didn't know how to respond, so I just said: 'What are you talking about?' I honestly don't know how I managed to stay upright.

We were given a load of forms and papers to sign that went into excruciating detail about every possible risk Ellie faced during the operation, from the anaesthetic to the surgery itself. I felt as if I was signing her – and my – life away.

That night, Ellie and I stayed at Great Ormond Street and Mark stayed at a hotel right next door. I didn't really sleep. All the new information the nurse had given us just rattled around in my head. There had been so many risks listed on the form. I played through a million different scenarios where something terrible would happen to my baby. I had never felt stress like it.

The next morning, a team of nurses got Ellie ready for the gruelling ten-hour surgery. At around 10 a.m. we walked her into the theatre. I held her in my arms and gently placed her down into a little incubator bed. We stayed with her while they put her to sleep, and then we left the room. The sight of the oxygen mask swamping her delicate face broke my heart. I just remember crying at the thought of leaving my helpless child to face that ordeal without me. It doesn't feel like twenty years ago – the memory is still so fresh.

We were told to go away for eight or nine hours, although she was in there for more like ten in the end. Under any other circumstances, a day together with no kids in London would have been a fun experience for me and Mark. But it was horrific. We couldn't relax. We walked the streets aimlessly and hardly said a word to each other. I couldn't focus on anything other than Ellie and what was happening to her at that moment in theatre. It was the silence that was the worst. I wanted someone from the hospital to call me every half-hour to tell me it was all going well, but of course they couldn't do that. We just had to wait and wander and wonder. And *wonder*.

At about 5 p.m. the hospital called and told us to come back in, and to head to a specific waiting room. We sat in that room for another couple of hours, grateful that we were closer to her, but anxious that we had been summoned without hearing any news. I didn't understand why they were taking so long to come and update us. I imagined the worst. I don't know if you've ever experienced something similar, but it's hard not to do so in a situation like that.

Eventually, someone did come and explain what was happening. Ellie's heart had struggled to kick back in after the bypass. It had been touch and go, and the doctors had been afraid they were going to lose her. But she had pulled through. It was at that moment that I finally felt as if my own heart had started beating again. She was a fighter. And she was my strength, too.

They took us through to see her, and despite the preparation from the night before, it was a difficult sight. They had cut down the front of her chest, so her entire top half was in dressing and plaster. It felt as if there were a million wires and tubes coming out of her, and some were sticking out of her nose and mouth. There was a small strip of tape over each of her eyes to keep them shut. They're doing wonderful things on that ward, but the sight of all those children fighting for their lives – with the constant buzz and hum and beeps coming from each bed – made it unbearable. I felt more overwhelmed than I'd ever felt before.

We were told that the first forty hours after the operation were crucial, so we went to a flat near Great Ormond Street to try and rest. In reality, we spent the night staring at the phone, praying it wouldn't ring – but feeling that, at any moment, it might. She made it through the night, and then the whole forty-hour high-risk period. She stayed in intensive care for a week and a half before being moved to a high-dependency ward. Even when she was barely conscious, Ellie kept pulling the tubes out of her arm, so she ended up with extra holes where they had to replace them. She was stubbornly fighting for her life – but also fighting to be free from those wires!

I continued my stay in the flat by the hospital. It had been set up especially for families of children who were receiving care. Mark stayed for the first week, but had to nip back home to Ilford, Essex, now and again. We had to juggle childcare for Amy with different friends and family members. We made it work because we had to. My mum was a godsend, and she brought Amy to London to see us regularly. It felt as if we were living in our own little bubble world between the hospital and the flat. While everyone else was getting on with normal life, having fish fingers for tea and dropping their kids off for swimming after school, our world had completely changed, and it felt as if it would never be normal again. We had a new normal now.

To this day, I don't understand why we weren't told sooner about the full nature of the problems Ellie was facing and all the different things they would have to do during the operation. It came as a shock. But other than that, the doctors, nurses and every member of hospital staff were exceptional. The kindness we felt over the three weeks Ellie was receiving her care meant the world to us – and better than that, the procedure was successful. We were told that, for this type of operation, they expected her to need follow-up surgery, but that didn't happen. My little fighter struck once again!

Ellie still has a scar on her chest from the surgery. When she came home from that operation all those years ago, she got an infection where they had made the incision, so the scar she was left with was bigger than we'd hoped. But it's part of her story, and it hasn't affected her confidence.[1] It's a constant reminder that our scars can prove our strength.

The operation, and the weeks and months of recovery that followed, took their toll. That day walking around London, waiting for news, will remain one of the worst of my life. But once Ellie got the all-clear, something lifted. I felt for the first time that I could allow myself to be hopeful. I was finally able to stop focusing on the conditions Ellie had, and start focusing on Ellie herself. I wanted to get to know her, and connect and bond with her. I wanted to know what her personality was like and discover her character. And what a lot of character she turned out to have!

---

1   Ellie: Nope, never. Not at all.

6

Sister act

Amy's story

I'm Amy, Ellie's older sister. I was seven years old when she was born. I was desperate for a little brother or sister, just like my friends. I think I felt lonely – I wanted what so many other kids in my class had. Even though I was young, I remember giving up on the idea and just thinking it wasn't going to happen. Of course, at that age I had no idea what was going on, and I didn't realise my parents were trying to have another baby.

I was at home when Mum came to tell me she was pregnant. It was at our old house, and I can still picture myself sitting in the lounge, trying to soak in the news. I was excited, but it was a lot to take in after hoping for it for so long. The pregnancy passed me by in a blur, and it felt like it was really quick – although I'm sure it didn't feel like that for Mum!

When Mum went into labour, I stayed with my grandma. It was December and I was performing in my school nativity. I wasn't a main character or anything. I was shy as a child, so never wanted to take centre stage... unlike my sister! But Dad still came to watch me. I remember him speaking to me after the show and saying, 'Mum's had the baby.' I went to see Ellie when she was born, but I can't remember much of that trip.

It was two months later that Mum and Dad sat me down to tell me Ellie had Down syndrome. I hadn't noticed anything different about Ellie, but I knew Mum was going to a special group with other parents who had children with additional needs, and I didn't understand. I remember pestering her and asking why she needed to go.

Finally, they sat me down at our dining table and told me the news. I know I cried, but I'm not sure know why. I didn't understand what Down syndrome was or what it meant for our family; I just knew it was something serious from the way they were speaking to me. Mum explained that Ellie's chromosomes were different, but I didn't know what that meant. She said Ellie might not be able to walk or talk, and that she would need an operation at some point. I just felt really upset.

The heart operation felt like the scariest part, because we really didn't know if Ellie would make it through. I could tell my parents were trying to gently prepare me for the fact that there was a fifty per cent chance I wouldn't see her again.

Mum arranged a family photoshoot before Ellie went into hospital. She said she wanted pictures of the four of us together as a family, just in case the worst happened. We all wore matching outfits – it sounds silly now that I think about it, but it was very sweet. I wore a black vest top and jeans, and Ellie wore a baby version of the same.

During Ellie's operation, I stayed with my grandma. I was with her for two weeks, which felt like a lifetime to a seven-year-old. Grandma took me up to Great Ormond Street Hospital after we found out the surgery had been successful, so we could visit Ellie. Ellie was in an incubator and there were loads of tubes coming out of her tiny body. I remember feeling scared by it all. It took me a couple of hours to get used to the sight of it, and to go over and see her. It was a relief when they finally discharged her from the hospital and the four of us were allowed back home.

I didn't feel like Ellie was at all different growing up. Even when I watch back the videos of us playing as children, it was all just so normal. She was fun and inquisitive, just like any other kid. I used to drive Mum a bit mad with my friends, though. Once Ellie had got to three or four years old, we started playing dress-up with her. We've got hundreds of photos where we did Ellie's hair and make-up, and she absolutely loved it. It was like having our very own doll!

I remember Mum getting frustrated when the school constantly blamed Ellie for things that went wrong. The teachers weren't the only ones, either. Once I was at a friend's house after school, and I overheard a couple of mums chatting in the kitchen. They didn't know I was listening and they were talking about Ellie. I could hear them listing all the things my sister would never be able to do. They were commenting on how she wouldn't walk and would never go to a 'normal' school. I felt heartbroken that my precious baby sister was the subject of gossip. I went home and told my mum, and she was furious.

Once I got to secondary school, my friends absolutely loved Ellie. They still do! None of my mates said anything negative about her, and they were obsessed with her bubbly character. Little did I know where that bubbly character would take her.

7

Expectation versus reality

Back to Ellie...

From what Mum has said, it seems the doctors – especially the ones who were there when I was born – didn't expect me to make much of my life. They said I wouldn't walk or talk, but Mum says once I got better after my heart operation I was really alert. My eyes were constantly looking around the room, taking in everything I saw.

Growing Hope's Naomi Graham says that the charity sees 'seemingly impossible' changes with almost every family who comes to them, and I love that it happened for us, too. Naomi told me and Mum a story about a ten-year-old boy called Sam. He had meningitis when he was two, and was left with a learning disability and a physical disability afterwards.

One thing he found really tricky was tying his shoelaces. The charity worked with him for six weeks, and by the fifth week he still hadn't managed to tie his laces. He had to practise all the time to get used to doing it, and he dreaded it because it was so tough for him. After lots of encouragement and more support, he proudly showed them by the sixth week that he could do it! It sounds small, but it's not at all. It meant he could play football without being embarrassed if his laces came undone. When you're convinced you can't do something because that's what people have said, and then you finally manage it, it's the best feeling in the world.

It took me a bit longer to learn things than it did for Amy and for other kids, but I found my own way of dealing with challenges. I never crawled – but who needs to when you're the master of the bum shuffle? It's like a twerk, but while you're sitting on the ground – and believe me, it got me places just as quickly as the normal way on all fours!

I was two when I actually managed to take steps and walk around on two feet, and that's when the talking kicked in, too. I may have been a late starter, but believe me when I tell you, I made up for lost time! To begin with I communicated with a combination of words and Makaton – the simple form of sign language. One of the first things I learned how to sign was 'more cake'. I was pretty good at any sentence that involved food, to be honest! I still remember some of it now, although these days if I want more cake I just go to Costa.

The Makaton helped me to express myself when I was still working out which words to put where. As my speech got better and better, I stopped needing to use it as much. I wasn't offered any speech therapy, so Mum and Dad saved up to send me to have some privately. Saying words clearly was a bit of a challenge for me, and sometimes I still have to repeat things a few times if people are not used to my voice. But that's a small price to pay when people thought I would never be able to say a single word. Imagine that… I wouldn't have been able to order cake!

I think it was around then, when I was two, that Mum and Dad realised I wasn't going to be as limited as they had thought. Once they could see me making progress, possibilities opened up – like going to mainstream schools and nurseries, and doing activities and making friends. They suddenly realised that if I'd already achieved more than the doctors thought, what else could I go on to do? They still had to take one day at a time, but things were looking up.

Have you ever exceeded expectations like that? Have you ever proved people wrong when they were convinced you couldn't do something? I bet we all have, even if we don't know it. It feels really good. It makes me feel proud, and you should feel proud of yourself, too. Let's live a life without limits – no matter what other people say we can and can't do!

8

Nursery

Now we're getting to the stuff that I was actually old enough to remember. Well, I say I remember, but I was quite young at nursery. So this is probably a combination of what I remember and what I *think* I remember, because they've become classic family stories that we tell from time to time. But that's how all the best childhood memories are made, right?

I loved nursery. For me, the whole experience was positive. I was happy and a bit cheeky – pretty much how I am now. And I was obsessed with books. I wanted to read constantly. I don't know how I got so good at reading, but I did quickly. I think I might have taught myself to read, and then I just wouldn't put them down. I would play with the magnetic letters on the fridge to recreate the words I'd learnt at nursery when I was at home.

When Mum saw me doing fridge spelling, she went out and bought those magnets with whole words on, and I would muddle them around, making my own sentences. I would even pick up Dad's newspaper and try to say the words on the black and white pages. I never sounded words out like you're supposed to; I would just say the word as it popped into my head. Mum said it was very weird,[1] but here we are almost two decades on and I'm telling my story in an entire book!

I was also really into dressing up. I had a full rail of fancy dress outfits that I could put on and play at being fun characters. Little did I know that in the future someone would be paying me to wear gorgeous clothes for a living. Thank goodness I got in all that early practice!

---

1 Yvonne: I literally have no idea where she picked it up from!

30

I went to two mainstream nurseries – one from the age of two-and-a-half, and the other from when I was three. I went to the first nursery three days a week. Mum tried to get me in there for the whole week, but they wouldn't increase the time they could offer me. I think they probably weren't prepared for kids with additional needs, and they didn't really know what to do with me. You see, I had a lot of energy, and at times I could get pretty hyperactive. I was just so excited to be around the other kids, and to play and read with them. But the nursery had never had a child with Down syndrome before, so it wasn't just me who had a lot to learn. Mum says they needed staff who were better trained and qualified in working with children with different needs.

They definitely thought I was a bit naughty. I had a lot of character and, like any child at that age, I was trying to figure out how the world worked. Sometimes that meant I was a little badly behaved, but aren't all children like that? I was desperate to read the books, so a few times I slipped them into my bag, wanting to take them home and read them in my room that night. But when the nursery realised this they were very upset and called Mum in.[2]

I think they saw me as a problem. They didn't really stop to notice my passions and talents. Mum said they were always very negative about me and didn't focus on my positives. But I still liked them, and I liked being there. I wasn't frustrated, I was too young to notice, but I know Mum was really bothered by the way they cared for me.[3] Sometimes it's easier to get annoyed on behalf of someone you care about than for yourself, isn't it? I suppose Mum is right that they could have taken the time to learn more about me and what I was good at, rather than writing me off as 'the girl with Down syndrome'. Mum says everyone babied me, which if I'm honest I didn't mind, but I suppose it didn't push me to progress as much as I could have.

---

2   Yvonne: It was so frustrating when they said that Ellie was 'stealing'. She wasn't a thief, just a child who didn't fully understand how things worked yet.

3   Yvonne: I felt that Ellie's intelligence was totally overlooked. She was treated as a stereotype, not a unique child.

I was three-and-a-half when I played my first prank. Well, I wouldn't have called it a prank myself, but it did give Mum and Amy a good scare. Amy was about ten at the time, and we were in Romford walking down the high street. I was in my buggy. (Mum kept me in the pushchair till I was about five, because my muscles took time to develop and I got tired really easily.[4]) Usually, I would sit there, watching the world, but this day was to be my great escape. I've always been double-jointed so, while Mum and Amy were looking in a jewellery shop window, I slipped out of my chair and broke free. They had been chatting away, but when Amy turned back from the window she looked at the buggy and said, 'Mum! Where's Ellie?'

I had completely disappeared, and suddenly there was a massive fuss as they ran around trying to find me. They pushed the empty buggy up and down the road, shouting my name. They ran through the shopping centre, peering into shops and asking strangers on the street if they'd seen a little girl. Mum says it was terrible. It probably felt the way I do when I think I've lost my phone… but way, way worse. After ten minutes – which isn't very long, but Mum says felt like a lifetime – Amy went into the same jeweller's where they'd been looking at necklaces in the window, and there I was. I was sitting on one of their fancy cushioned chairs, talking to the lovely ladies in the store.[5]

Even now when we walk past that jeweller's in town, I'll wind Mum up and pretend I'm slipping off to hide in there. I don't think she loves that joke, though! I was so flexible I could squeeze out of anything. Mum would buckle me into the car seat, and then look round a few minutes later to find that I'd squirmed free and was sitting on one of the normal chairs next to it. Even when I was really young, I wouldn't let anything hold me back – and I've kept going that way ever since.

---

4   Yvonne: She would sit in her pram bolt upright, looking around – like she was the Queen.

5   Yvonne: Yes, the lovely ladies who didn't think to pop their heads out of the shop and ask whether anyone had lost their kid!

9

The best things to do with friends

It took me a little while to make good friends when I started school, but once we all got to know each other I had great mates to play with at break times. We would have a laugh together doing all sorts of things, even though we sometimes fell out.

Here are some of my favourite things to do when I'm hanging out with friends. These may sound like simple things, but I think it's sometimes good to stop and remember the little things that can make up a wonderful, big and hopeful life, such as:

1 Holding someone's hand if they get upset.
2 Sleepovers where you stay up and talk all night.
3 Going to local clubs, like drama or dance.
4 Pyjama parties – even if you're much older than I was back then!
5 Dancing around the living room (again, no age limit).
6 Hanging out in the garden. It's always good to get out into nature.
7 Watching films (and rewatching your favourites over and over again).
8 Going to parties. Some people want to leave early – I do *not*.

10

Advice for mums

More from Yvonne

Ellie and I know that a lot of different people will read this book, and some of them will be parents, carers and loved ones who are worried about the children in their own lives (and if you don't fit into that camp, you'll know someone who does – so this chapter will hopefully still be helpful to you). Some of those children may have Down syndrome, like Ellie, while others may just be struggling in a way that their parents weren't expecting and weren't prepared for. I think all parents worry a lot about their kids, don't they? I know I did with Amy. No matter what happens, and how good your baby's medical health is, being a parent hits you like a train. There's never a moment when you don't worry about your children.

Being a first-time mum to Amy was tough and exhausting, but filled with joy and bursting with love. Being a mum to Ellie was exactly the same. The first few years were the hardest but, just like parenting any child, it gets easier and more manageable. Even now, I still have to remember that I'm taking it one day at a time, just as Mark said on that first day. It's so important for me to focus on that next step, and often I turn around and realise just how far I've come.

If you're reading this because you're facing a situation you weren't expecting, one that feels too hard and you need some hope, let me give you the encouragement I know I needed on that first awful day at the hospital. You can do this. It will be tough, but *you're* tough. And if you don't feel tough, you'll quickly realise how tough you are. Because you're going to have to be. This will not feel unmanageable forever, or even for very long.

No one can ever know the outcome of any situation. We had no idea what kind of life Ellie would have. With the heart condition, we weren't even sure Ellie would get to have a life at all. To fully understand and process that situation was completely impossible in those early days. I just had to try to find some peace and calm in the confusion.

If your child has Down syndrome, they're not signing up to an awful life. Just a different one. If you haven't been given enough support and information, I'm sorry. Medical teams are wonderful, but they are busy and rushed, and they don't always get it right. A leaflet isn't enough to help you work this all out, so if nothing's volunteered, you'll need to be proactive. There are charities that will give you all the information you need. I've relied on the Down's Syndrome Association's website (mentioned in chapter 2). It's so helpful. There are groups and activities, especially for children with Down syndrome, and plenty of wonderful mainstream clubs that will welcome your child and make adaptations where needed.

Working as a team is key. If you have a partner, the two of you need to communicate well and support each other. Otherwise, it's a case of gathering family, friends, teachers and medical professionals around you to make sure you're on the same page. My relationship with Mark changed when Ellie came along. It had to change because *we* changed. We faced new stresses, and we stopped planning ahead – just dealing with each day as it came.

No one will understand how your life has changed unless they have their own child in the same position, and even then it can feel isolating. Early on in our journey with Ellie I met a friend who also had a child with Down syndrome, and that was really special. We met once a month for lunch on our own. It's so important to speak to someone who gets it, without having to explain the context or fill in the medical gaps. We also have to remember not to compare the progress of our children with others, particularly with Down's. Every child is unique, and each child's progress is different.

We raised our Ellie just as we had raised our Amy. We never assumed she couldn't do something, even if some things took a bit longer for her than for other children. I had to resist people who put her in a box because of the Down syndrome, but I had to make sure that I wasn't putting her in a box either. I've found people have been quick to dismiss Ellie, either because it's too much hard work to dig deeper and really get to know her or because they assume they know everything just by looking at her. As her mum, it's always been my job to encourage her to try again or keep going, especially if other people around her have decided she can't. No child with Down syndrome can be categorised by the condition. They have different abilities in different areas; different interests and passions that develop and grow as they do.

Ellie has done amazingly well, but it's been a long road made up of tiny steps. I burst with pride whenever I think about what she's achieved. My mum was always convinced Ellie would make something of herself, but we were too focused on the present to imagine what the future might look like. The darkest days were definitely those first ones, when we felt confused and lost at the hospital, but each new stage of Ellie's life has brought new challenges. During her school years, Mark and I had to remind ourselves once again to take each challenge as it came. Perhaps you need to remind yourself of the same today.

11

Starting school

Ellie only ever went to a mainstream primary school, which meant there wasn't any specialist care. Norah Myers went to a mainstream school and found that she was bullied a lot because of her cerebral palsy. Looking back, she told us she wishes she had grown up more integrated into the disability community because she would have met other people who understood what she was going through.

It was a hard choice for me and Mark to make, but we felt mainstream school was the best place for Ellie to grow and learn. Ellie really enjoyed the school and made some great friends, so it just shows that not everyone with disabilities has the same experience, and each person needs to be treated as an individual. Our decision didn't come without resistance, though.

Other parents were upset that we had sent Ellie to the school, and they didn't make much effort to hide it from me. Sometimes I would overhear nasty comments in the playground about how she shouldn't be there alongside the able-bodied children. Another mum came right over to me once and told me Ellie should be in a 'special school'. I know not everyone will agree with us, but we knew Ellie, and we knew that she was best off exactly where she was.

Early years expert Alistair Bryce-Clegg said that the key to more inclusive parenting is awareness, so maybe they just weren't very aware. Parents are so desperate to do what's right for their kids that they can get sucked in by all the advice on the internet. Some of it is very useful, but some is just fearmongering.

Alistair told me that he tries to get parents up to date with 'realistic parenting' rather than all the Instagram perfection and the forums, which can be hostile at times. He also said that parents and children would benefit from more diverse representation in our media, as it would help everyone to become more familiar with uniqueness, and therefore bring more understanding and acceptance of it. I'm proud that Ellie's playing her part in that now. Hopefully, it will make a difference in the way parents respond to others in their children's classes.

Worse than the parents was the headteacher, who did everything she could to have Ellie removed. She constantly called us with complaints of reasonably minor behavioural problems that were normal for a child with Down syndrome. Any bit of damage at the school was blamed on Ellie. It always felt as if the head was mounting evidence so she could build a case for Ellie to be expelled. She wasn't successful, but that's because we fought back.

Ellie could be a handful – of course I knew that. I'm her mum! But she wasn't malicious or harmful, just excitable and mischievous. It was hard to see her so misunderstood and afforded so little patience. My suspicions about the headteacher were confirmed when Ellie left the school and we were handed all her paperwork for our records. In among the reports and forms, they had left in a letter from the headteacher addressed to the council. She was petitioning them to take Ellie out of the school. She described her as 'dangerous' and said she had mental health issues. I felt so disappointed as I read this official letter. It was such a blow. I couldn't believe she had so openly discriminated against our child.

Alistair Bryce-Clegg was a headteacher as well as an early-years consultant, and when we spoke to him, he said he had a very inclusive whole-school ethos and actively supported children with additional needs attending mainstream schools. I'm sad that I didn't receive the same welcome from Ellie's school.

Alistair has found that while everyone's experience is different, there are factors that make supporting the needs of a child with Down syndrome easier. For example, it helps if the teachers and learning support staff are experienced in working with people with Down's, and if the parents or carers are proactive in giving the school information and resources that support the child's need. He claims it is important to acknowledge that children with Down syndrome can be very different from one another, so there cannot be a one-size-fits-all approach.

Despite all this, Ellie was happy at primary school. We didn't tell her about everything that happened behind closed doors; it wouldn't have been right to.

A huge reason that Ellie had such a good time and grew so much while she was there came down to her support worker, Evette.[1] Evette spent virtually every day with Ellie from reception to year six, and they became so close they were practically family. I'll leave her to fill in the primary school gaps – because it wasn't all bad. Far from it.

---

1 Ellie: Evette was my primary school mum!

12

Mischievous at primary school

Evette's story

I was fortunate enough to be Ellie's learning support assistant (LSA) throughout primary school, and I've got some great stories from that time. There was never a dull moment with Ellie! I've always called her 'my Ellie'.[1] I joke with my husband that we have five children, not four, because I spent so much time with Ellie when she was growing up that I think of her as family. It was a great blessing to have such consistency.

I was one of two support staff who was with Ellie from her fourth day at school until the April that she was in year six. It was me and another LSA called Michelle. I did all the academics and the paperwork with Ellie, while Michelle focused on the glitter and the art and all the fun things. Children need a lot of support and one-to-one attention in their first five years. That's when they learn the most vital skills that will set them up for life. Being able to focus on Ellie's care meant that I got to understand all the complex and unique elements of her development. I got to know her so well that I understood all her quirks and character traits. She had a lot of character – even as a young girl.

I clearly remember the first day I met Ellie. She'd been in the reception class for four days and her LSA had already walked out. She just put her hands up and said, 'I can't cope.' Ellie needed someone who could match her strong will, and sadly the young woman they assigned to the job was not ready for Ellie. Even though she was only four years old, Ellie ran rings around her, and

---

1   Evette: It's actually more 'MyEllie' said as just one word!

apparently spent those first few days causing chaos in the classroom and ignoring everything she was told.

I knew straight away that she was independent and full of energy, and that would never change – and quite rightly, too. I'm pleased she never lost that glint in her eye. The thing is, this strong will needed to be channelled in the right direction, and that was my job. They pulled me out of the year-six class where I was supporting a young lad I'd worked with for four years and introduced me to Ellie Goldstein. The headteacher just told me I was in charge and left me to it. I didn't know it then, but that's when the adventure started.

The best word I can use to describe Ellie is 'firecracker'. She was such a livewire. I could see why the teachers found her a challenge. In those early days she would be furious if she couldn't do something. I would set her a challenge and she would get so frustrated if she didn't get it straight away that she would literally sweep everything off the tables nearby. She would scribble on people's notebooks and once picked up her chair and threw it to the ground. Her speech was still developing, so it was hard for her to express herself, and it would just burst out. But I got that. I'm sure none of us would deal well with finding something difficult and not being able to explain ourselves.

It took a while for people to understand what Ellie was saying. I got used to chatting with her very quickly, so I didn't have any trouble understanding, but it wasn't like that with everyone. People who didn't spend as much time with her had to get used to her pronunciation, which took a little effort, and some people didn't bother to put that effort in at all. Her Makaton skills were phenomenal, though. She could have given Mr Tumble a run for his money! She slowly stopped using it as her speech improved, but Ellie's memory is so good that it wouldn't surprise me at all if she still remembers some.[2]

Another thing that was totally astonishing about Ellie was that she was really good at reading at such a young age. She was well

---

2   Ellie: I do, actually. I still know how to say 'cake'.

above the others in her class, and she absolutely loved it. She could recite any story, fairy tale or nursery rhyme. She knew all about the characters and their plot lines. The more time I spent with her, the more it became clear that she was highly intelligent. Maybe that's why she found the stumbling blocks so frustrating – because she *did* understand and knew she was capable.

When Ellie decided she couldn't do something, her default was to cause trouble instead; from screaming to running out of the classroom. She was bright enough to recognise that she had limitations at times. You see, Ellie would panic and go into fight or flight mode when things got difficult (I imagine many people reading this who don't have Down's can relate). She would either try to get away, or scream and lash out. Sometimes that could be destructive and very distracting for the other pupils.

I remember on one occasion Ellie was shocked because one of her friends was sick in class. She struggled to process what was happening, so she started screaming. The teacher was furious and shouted at her in front of everyone. Ellie recently brought this up with me, all these years later, and said how naughty she had been. But I had to tell her that she wasn't being naughty or bad – she was just frightened. That was her way of reacting.

Sometimes she felt overwhelmed by everything around her, and you could see the cogs whirring in her brain. Then she'd just go into overdrive, overwhelmed by all the inputs swirling around in her head. It probably didn't help that she was so perceptive – probably more so than a 'normal' child of her age. She noticed *everything*. And sometimes that was too much, and it led to what some people deemed 'bad behaviour'.

She certainly wasn't evil, and she definitely wasn't bad. She was kind and enthusiastic; it just took her a while to adjust to different environments and to learn to keep calm as she worked it all out. But she moved well past that stage as she grew up at school. I think it's really important for you (*you*, reading this right now) to know that for those 'difficult children' with disabilities, learning problems or behavioural issues, their current challenges don't mean they'll struggle forever. As they get older and move towards adulthood, many of those reactions and responses can be channelled in a good and productive way. Ellie is proof of that.

Still, Ellie had a lot to navigate at school, Like her speech, her writing took longer to develop than for many other children. I used to act as a scribe for her, and she was also given a computer – long before every classroom was packed full of them! Ellie wanted to be friends with everyone, but some children seemed wary, like they didn't know how to play with her.

Before your heart starts to break as you imagine four-year-old Ellie with no friends in the playground, stop right there. It may have taken a while for Ellie and the other children to get used to each other, but kids adapt quickly. Ellie had a lovely group of boys and girls she played with, and they grew up together over the years. They really got to know and understand her. I would go out into the playground with her and teach her how to play well and share with the others, and she was a fantastic friend – with fantastic friends.

The other children liked her because she had a good heart. She was always the first to help someone up if they fell over. She would always volunteer to take someone to see the school nurse. She was kind, caring and very nurturing – and she still is.

It was the school itself that took a bit longer to adapt. Ellie was its first student with Down's, and it was a steep learning curve. In those days, many schools didn't really want special needs children in a mainstream environment. Each class had thirty or so children, and the teachers would be angry if Ellie found something so tough that she had a meltdown. I understood that it made it hard to teach the others in the class, so I often took Ellie out, and a lot of the time it was just the two of us. Sometimes it was easier for us to find a separate space to practise Ellie's maths than cooped up at the back of the classroom. I think that one-on-one time is what helped us develop such a special bond.

None of these troubles affected Ellie. You've got to remember that, when it comes to Ellie, her personal perception of situations is probably very different from yours. If the two of you were walking down the street and you stopped to chat to someone who was a bit

rude to you both, she would take that interaction completely differently from how you would. She might think that they weren't that
rude after all. So Ellie loved school. Loved, loved, loved it. She had
the absolute best time.

13

Mischievous out and about

If I learned anything quickly, it was that Ellie desperately needed boundaries. She needed to learn the 'rules of the world' (especially given the high-powered spaces and places she'd find herself in just a few short years later), which other people just seemed to grasp naturally. She needed help understanding the structures we live in and how best to navigate them. I put firm boundaries in place, and she responded really well to them.

One thing I didn't have to teach Ellie was how to go after what she wanted. She had everyone else wrapped around her little finger. If I wasn't there, she was so clued up that she knew she could get what she wanted from other people. I was always amused to come back from a day off to find out how she had pushed her luck this time.

Once, someone from the council's outreach team – an expert who was there to make sure Ellie was well looked after – came to visit us. The woman took Ellie to the school library. I had agreed with Ellie that she could take out one book at a time, so should pick her favourite to bring back. Next thing I know, Ellie's proudly strutting down the corridor with the outreach worker carrying a stack of ten books. I couldn't believe my eyes! When I asked what had happened, the poor out-of-her-depth outreach worker said, 'She just wanted them.'

Well, I bet she did! Of course, this was no big deal – we could just drop them back at the end of the day. But it wasn't about the books. It was about her understanding of the social cues. I knew that the better she was socially, the more opportunities she would have in life. If people kept letting her get away with things, it wouldn't help her in the long run.

I now work at a school with autistic children, and helping them to develop socially is the biggest challenge but the most valuable process. So much is 'said' non-verbally, and I didn't want Ellie to miss out on that. She said I was strict, and I definitely was. But I loved watching her develop and seeing her finally 'get it'. That's why I started a new scheme to help Ellie grow in a range of different environments. It was called the Out and About Programme.

I petitioned the headteacher to let me take Ellie out of school once a week. Yvonne gave her permission to do so, and we would go on a day trip to the high street every Friday. In those days the paperwork wasn't so strict, but I did write my own risk assessment to make sure we had thought through all the possibilities (I'd heard about her Houdini antics in the early years). For each trip, we kept a diary of where we had gone and what we had learned.

Our first official Out and About trip was to the library. It was a natural first choice because, as we know, Ellie loved books, and I wanted to teach her how to borrow them. I wanted her to know that people would want to lend things to her, but she had to ask, and it had to be done in the right way. The books then needed to be looked after and returned by the deadline.

It was touch and go at first. Ellie would always try to run out of the library – sometimes with a book in her hands and sometimes without. I would have to pelt down the hall and stop her before she got to the door, with everyone in the silent library staring at us for disturbing their peace.

One day I told her, 'If you run out and make it to the door, the shutters are going to go down and we're going to get stuck in here.' Everyone who raises children tells these little white lies for their own good, don't they? I'm sure more than one of us has faked a phone call to the 'police' before! Whether you agree with the tactics or not, she got the message – thank goodness. She started to look forward to scanning the book she had chosen and walking out of the library, rather than making a break for it.

As the scheme had proved successful, we started bringing one or two other children out with us on our trips to the high street so they could develop their life skills. That was fun for Ellie, although a bit harder work for me and the teachers. It meant that she could spend time with her peers, and it became a social activity. Ellie and the others would suggest where we went next, and they got excited about the outings.

Every now and again, Yvonne would give Ellie a bit of money, just 50p or £1, to spend while we were out. This meant I could show Ellie the process of buying something, of speaking to the cashier, counting the change and then asking for a receipt. I always stressed to her how important it was not to leave the shop without a receipt. That way there would never be any mix-ups.

On one of these days, we went to the local charity shop. It had the usual rails of clothes, and bits and bobs of kitchenware, but at the back there were shelves and shelves of donated books. Ellie obviously headed straight to the back and started scanning the rows of books. She was excited that there were so many to choose from. She squealed as she pulled *Sleeping Beauty* and *Snow White and the Seven Dwarves* off the shelf and held them up. She said they were her absolute favourite stories. She told me she used to have them at home, but had looked for them recently and couldn't find them. She was really upset, but now she'd found these, so it was perfect. I helped her walk them up to the counter and pay for them – making sure she got her receipt.

Later that day, Yvonne came to collect Ellie, who excitedly explained the whole story before pulling the books out of her bag to proudly show her mum. The only problem was, Ellie hadn't lost those books. She had so many books that Yvonne had given some to the local charity shop. Ellie had just bought back her own books without realising! Yvonne couldn't be annoyed, it was far too funny. She just hung her head and laughed, admitting that she would probably never be able to shift the mountains of books Ellie had at home.

On another of these outings we headed to the Catholic charity shop in town. When we walked in, we saw a man behind the counter who had Down syndrome. It was the first time I'd been with Ellie when she had seen someone else with Down's in person, although she had been to groups and clubs with Yvonne. She didn't ever say that someone had Down syndrome; she just said they looked 'uncertain'. I don't know why. That was her word for it. If I showed her pictures of others with Down's, that was the word she used. It was all part of her working out the world. But when I asked her, Ellie never thought she looked 'uncertain' herself. It never occurred to her that she had any special needs at all. She was just Ellie Goldstein, and we didn't treat her any differently from anyone else.

Sometimes Michelle (my friend and Ellie's other LSA) would come with us into town. Michelle was the lenient one! On one of our days out we went into a coffee shop, and I ordered two coffees while Michelle and Ellie went to the corner shop next door to grab a newspaper. This was one of the days Ellie had some pocket money, so she wanted to get herself a treat. She always picked the same thing: a chocolate Freddo frog and a Ribena. They came back to the cafe, purchases in hand, and we sat and chatted while Ellie tucked into the chocolate, kicking off her shoes under the table (she absolutely hated having them on).

I suddenly realised there was a Freddo wrapper on the table and Ellie was about to open a second, but she had only been allowed to buy one. I asked her, 'How come you've got two Freddos?' She replied, 'Because I bought them.' I looked at Michelle, thinking maybe she had been played and Ellie had convinced her to let her have two. But she hadn't. Michelle said, 'No, you only paid for one Freddo.'

I looked in her coat and found a third Freddo hiding in there, and knew exactly what had happened. I marched her straight back to the newsagent and told her to explain what she had done, and then apologise. Then I made her hand them back. The kind man behind the counter immediately said, 'No, no, no! She can keep them, it's OK.' But I stood my ground and made her return both of the unpaid-for chocolate bars.

I get that people want to be nice to a young girl, particularly one with Down syndrome, but letting her keep them would have sent the wrong message. I was so desperate for her to be well respected in society. Lots of children pocket sweets from the shop, of course;

it's not just Ellie. But she already had so much to grasp which wouldn't come naturally to her that I wanted it to be a real lesson. Sadly, it wasn't the last time I had to teach Ellie this lesson, but on the next occasion I had a plan.

14

The long arm of the law

Whatever Ellie did with the school I was there with her, including school trips. Once we went off to Europe for three days, and on another, slightly less glam trip, we headed north to York. With its cobbled streets and quaint little shops, York looks like something out of Harry Potter. There was plenty planned for the excursion, and I stuck close to Ellie to make sure she was enjoying it and didn't feel overwhelmed. She had the best time ever. She was fantastic and so well behaved… until we went to walk the wall.

Around the perimeter of the city of York is an ancient wall. You can walk along it around the entire city if you want to, seeing the beauty of York from all angles. Ellie and her friends walked around it beautifully. We stayed towards the back so she would have space to walk, but there was no danger. It wasn't particularly narrow, and she definitely didn't want me to hold her hand – she was far too independent for that. Then, all of a sudden, she kicked her shoes off and threw them over the wall and onto the floor below. That's how Ellie could be sometimes: an absolute angel one moment and cheeky as anything the next.

On the same trip we were heading home when she pulled some finger puppets out of her bag and started to play with them. I was confused. I knew we hadn't packed finger puppets and they were brand new. I asked her where she got them from, but I already knew. She had taken them and popped them into her bag without being spotted by the owner of one of the tourist stalls. She confessed that she hadn't paid for them, but by this time we had travelled too far to go back and return them.

She knew she wasn't allowed to take them – she wasn't stupid, and I'd told her plenty of times before. But I realised she didn't understand that this wasn't just cheeky; it was very wrong and against the law. Lots of children do similar things, but I needed her to understand that it could cause big problems for her. Ellie's outlook on the world is that it's ultimately a nice place, where sometimes you're a bit mischievous and break the rules, but that people will let you off. I needed her to know that this wouldn't always be the case.

So, I turned her in to the police station.

All right, I've made that sound more dramatic than it actually was. I needed a plan – something that would scare her, so she'd be safe and stick to the rules from then on. When we got home I called the local police station in Essex. I told them all about Ellie; that she had Down syndrome and I was helping her to learn important skills, both in school and out. I told them she just couldn't understand how important it was for her not to take things that weren't hers. I asked if someone in uniform could speak to her, and they agreed. '*Bring her in!*'

On our next Out and About day I marched her into Barkingside Police Station, and they knew to expect her. I told her we had to go in to talk about the puppets. The police officers were brilliant. The officer – in his full gear, with the hat and the belt and the walkie-talkie – came out and explained that taking things that weren't hers without paying for them was very wrong. He stressed how bad it was, and that if someone stole a big thing or lots of things they would get into serious trouble, and they might end up in the police cells.

Ellie listened to every word. When he was finished, she said, 'I'm never going to take anything ever again!' She was definitely scared by what he had said to her. But I didn't want the whole experience to be negative, and neither did they. So once they were sure she had understood, Ellie got to sit in the police car and was allowed to press the button to turn on the siren. Even after confessing to taking the finger puppets, she still managed to charm the police. Honestly, you can't take her anywhere! To this day, I've never heard of her taking anything that wasn't hers again. She's also very diligent about collecting her receipt to make sure that, if a police officer ever asks, she can prove that she has paid.

These weren't the only memorable trips; we went on many. And what I've found is that Ellie is most engaged when she sees the relevance of what she is working on. When she can see how something slots into her life and her reality, she wants to know more about it. Museums didn't offer that insight for her. They didn't make her feel anything, so she completely switched off when we visited them. Sometimes she would just run towards the exit, eager to break for freedom from the dull exhibition in front of her. On occasion she would take off her shoes and hide them behind plinths and statues, creating a bit of fun for herself during a tour.

A trip to the Women's Museum turned out to be one of those days when Ellie was definitely not going to walk around quietly and pretend to be interested. I cut my losses and took her to a cafe nearby, hoping that sitting down and waiting for a piping hot chocolate to cool would give her time for the world in her head to calm down so we could go back and join the others. She was up and down and fidgeting a bit, but she did eventually settle. After we had finished our drinks, I gathered our things together so we could rejoin the tour – hopefully just in time to look around the gift shop. But then I realised, once again, that Ellie had no shoes on. I started frantically looking around on the booth seating and by the cabinet where the waiter had rung up our bill, and then I saw them: two worn children's size sevens in the window next to the strawberry tarts and chocolate eclairs. I was mortified. I whipped them out of the display and pushed them onto Ellie's little feet as quickly as I could before making a dash for the door.

Sometimes Ellie's attention would waver; not just in museums, but in class, too. She would run out of the room, and the teachers weren't always as patient as I would have liked. They would get annoyed and shout at her from time to time, which made her, them and me more frustrated. It didn't help anyone.

I learned that I had to be creative to get her excited about a task – particularly in maths, which was her worst subject. She would go through phases of being obsessed with one thing for a while. I remember when I was trying to help her get to grips with counting, she was in a period where she was fascinated by fire alarms. So

I walked her around the school counting fire alarms to help her grasp the idea. I even taught her directions, and her right and left, by drawing a map of the school corridors and asking her to direct us to the next fire alarm. She absolutely loved it.

No matter how many tactics I used, however, I could never get Ellie as excited about maths as she was about drama and dance. The girl was born to perform. Seeing her dance was such a joy. She picked up choreography instantly and threw herself into it. We tried to get her enrolled in a nearby drama club for children with disabilities. They were sadly fully booked, but she still loved every opportunity she was given to get on stage at school. It's a shame she never got into acting – she's so dramatic! Plus, her memory meant that she was excellent at learning a script. She must have a photographic memory, because I could never have learned things by heart the way she did.

The only thing I can't believe is that she is now a model – and not because she doesn't have the beauty or the confidence. Believe me, she has both of those things by the bucketload. It came as a surprise because she always used to tear her tights… and I don't even mean by accident! Sometimes I would turn away and then look back, and she would have pulled a huge hole in her tights. I feel sorry for any stylist who puts her in a pair, as she loves to push her fingers through the nylon and watch them ladder.

Ellie could be working at McDonald's or on the cover of *Vogue* and she'd be exactly the same. She's just Ellie. I'm so proud to see the woman she's become. She's successful, polite and kind. She is very skilled socially, and she listens. She's still a diva, but no one would ever want her to stop all the sass and hair flicking. It's who she is!

15

Daddy's girl

Ellie again...

All this talk about my mum and my teachers, and my poor dad hasn't had a look-in. So here's what you need to know about Dad. First, his name is Mark (I think you've probably got that by now!). Second, he's very handsome (you might have got that from looking at me!).[1]

Mum and Dad have been married for a long time; it will soon be their thirty-fifth wedding anniversary. They got married at a synagogue in Great Portland Street. Mum wore a big ivory princess dress with beads and diamonds,[2] and a massive bow on the back. Dad looked smart in a black suit with a bow tie. It was in 1988, so they look a bit funny in the pictures.

They met each other through friends. They were all young and hung out together at the pub or the disco, or wherever old people used to go to see their friends. Mum says it's all different these days.[3] She had heard about Dad before they met up – probably because he was so good-looking. A good friend of Mum's asked if she wanted to go on a blind double date and she said yes, but she had no idea who was going to show up. Of course, it was Dad!

I would say that Dad's the strong, silent type. Sometimes I think he's a bit shy around people, but he's really funny. Mum says he always made her laugh when they first met. With me he's strict,[4] but my favourite things to do with Dad are go to McDonald's or

---

1 Yvonne: Ha! Is he? (Only joking… he's all right.)

2 Yvonne: Well, they were diamantes not real diamonds!

3 Yvonne: No swiping or social media back in our day.

4 Yvonne: He's direct with you, Ellie, not strict!

to the fair in Southend with all the rides. Or even better, go to McDonald's in Southend and then to the fair! My order is always a Crispy Chicken Wrap or Chicken Selects with fries and either a Tropicana or a Fanta Orange. But I have to guard my chips to stop Dad from stealing them!

16

Ellie's best books

As you know by now, I *love* reading (although I've learned my lesson to always ask before I borrow books, and so should you!). I hope you're enjoying this book, but here are my absolute favourite other books to try out when you're finished. It may be that you've read some of these before, but I swear they will keep being good the second or third time around.

Snow White and the Seven Dwarfs (you can watch the movie, too)
The Horrid Henry series
Queen Elizabeth: A Platinum Jubilee celebration (I'm in this one!)
Sleeping Beauty
The Peppa Pig series (I haven't read these for a while, but I have such fond memories of them)
My English practice textbooks (not maths, that's rubbish!)
Any book by Jacqueline Wilson
The Drama Llama: A story about soothing anxiety

17

Secondary school

Secondary school was very different from primary school, but I don't mind when things change, and I always try to take new situations in my stride. I went to three different secondary schools. The first one was in Loughton, near where we lived. I remember walking into the building on the trial day and wondering how I would work out how to move around the school without getting lost. It was a mainstream school with 1,200 students and plenty of different departments and corridors and buildings. The trial day was to introduce all the pupils to their teachers and one another, and to help us find our way around the place. We played games to learn one another's names and had a tour of the school.

This time, instead of having one or two people help me in all my classes, there was a team of twenty LSAs. There were five or six who looked after me, and they would stay with me for half-day shifts before swapping. At first they walked around with me to make sure I made it to each class, but I got used to the colour-coded system for the different areas, so after six months they left me to find my own way. I liked it when they met me in the classrooms. It was nice to have independence like all my friends. The LSA would still sit with me and my friends at lunch, but I didn't mind that – it was always fun. I had school dinners, and the pasta pot with cheese was always my favourite.

On my birthday one year, the learning support team threw me a big surprise party. I loved it! There was a cake, and they blew up balloons and brought in presents. I got a chocolate bar, a colouring book and a set of colouring pens.

I loved the school trips we went on. They took me to see *Jumanji: The next level*, and I jumped out of my skin at the spiders bit. I hate spiders and it was so scary! My favourite thing we did was a trip to Harry Potter World, where we walked down Diagon Alley and through Gringotts Bank with the creepy goblins. I got to ride on a broom, and they took a brilliant picture of me flying around.

This secondary school was the first place where I was involved in sports. I tried out for boccia and was so excited when I found out I had made the team. Boccia is a lot like the French game that people play on holiday called 'bocce' or 'boules' or 'pétanque'. They play it at the Paralympics, and there are lots of other World Boccia events for people with physical disabilities. The game is played with soft leather balls that are coloured red or blue, and you throw them onto a hard surface. The team that wins is the one with its balls closest to the white ball after everyone has thrown their balls.

In the process of writing this book, I realised how playing this sport gave me a lot more confidence in my physical abilities. I recently spoke to David Smith OBE about it. David is the best boccia player – a Paralympic champion and world number one! His success at the Beijing 2008 Paralympics really put boccia on the map in the UK. If you watched the Paralympics, you might remember him for his colourful mohawk hairstyle, or maybe you'll know him for doing a doughnut manoeuvre on television talk show *The Last Leg*. He started playing at school, when he was seven, but people told him he would never be any good at sport because of his disability. He definitely proved them wrong!

Early in my life, people said I would never walk, but David's experience was the other way around. People were constantly trying to get him to walk, even though it was very painful and he was comfortable with his electric wheelchair. He told us he just wanted people to see that he didn't need 'fixing', but rather he needed people to accept him as he was and help him achieve what he wanted to achieve. He said that social activities are really important in helping those with additional needs. He went to an amazing school for people with disabilities called Treloar and he got involved in drumming, hockey, football, navigation, driving (once he was old enough!), events, acting, writing and politics – he was even head boy! He wasn't wrapped up in cotton wool, and people challenged him. He said that boccia was so inclusive that it really built up his confidence. It did the same for me.

I was really good at it. Even the first time I tried, I had a knack for throwing. I know it's not a conventional sport, but it was fun to find something I could play well. We would go to other schools for competitions and sometimes we even won. The trick is to make sure your ball goes high enough that it lands near the white ball – although you don't want it to go too high. I loved the social side of playing a sport and hanging around with all my teammates.

Once we were playing against another team and it was my turn to go. I took my ball in my hand and stood at the line to make my throw. I was trying to get it to the right height, so I took a breath and then threw it into the air. But I got it completely wrong! The ball flew up way too high and didn't go anywhere near where I was aiming. Instead, it hit one of my teammates in the face... in the eye, actually. I didn't know what to do, so in my panic I just started laughing! Sometimes when I don't know how to react, it feels like all I can do is laugh. I felt so bad when I saw that he was upset, and then started to cry. Thankfully, he was all right in the end and wasn't properly hurt. There weren't any bruises the next day. We can laugh about it now – even though it was worrying at the time.

At school I loved drama (of course!) and history classes, but I still struggled with maths. When I got into year nine, I found the work in all my classes harder. The LSAs were amazing. The lessons were an hour and a half, so they made sure I got regular five-minute breaks to step outside and have a breather or a glass of water, otherwise I would just fidget. But even with the breaks it was difficult for me to cope when the work was faster-paced.

When I got frustrated or didn't understand, I would try to get out of the class. I could tell the teachers were finding it tough, and I know I was hard work. I got a lot of detentions. In detention you just had to sit there and do your homework quietly. It wasn't bad, it was just boring. Sometimes I would take books to read in detention and I really enjoyed that, but overall I would walk out of the session and think, 'Thank goodness it's over. I don't want to do that again.'

Once I got badly told off for swearing at one of the teachers. I was in a geography lesson and the teacher asked me to read a word from the board. I couldn't read it, so instead I shouted, 'What the f***?!' I can't remember what the word on the board was, but I know the teacher got really upset. I don't like to swear – I know it's not good – but I don't think I realised how upset the teacher would get.

It was a big school, so I overheard all sorts of things in the corridors and often knew when a word was bad – but that didn't mean I knew *why* it was. No one ever explained it to me. They just told me off when I got it wrong. In reality, I would only use those words when I was frustrated and didn't know how else to express myself. But of course they had to tell me off. They couldn't give me special treatment when any other pupil would have got in trouble. It would have set a bad example. The teacher called the senior leadership team and they gave me a detention.

Overall, it was a great school. It was strict and I couldn't get away with a lot – but Mum always said that was a good thing. I stayed until the end of year nine, but after that they started working towards GCSEs and they couldn't offer any other exams. I was already feeling stressed with the work, so Mum and Dad decided it was time to move me to another school.

The next school I went to was for children with mild-to-moderate learning disabilities. It was a very different place. The building was much smaller, so it was very easy to find my way around – and there were only a few hundred students. Even though I had loved my old school, I wasn't sad to move. I felt confident and was looking forward to making new friends. I don't think too much about change, I just get on with it. Mum says that some people really struggle with it – maybe you are one of them – but generally speaking, I try to look ahead with positivity.

One change I didn't like was my new uniform. The grey skirt and navy cardigan were fine, but at my old school we had worn a shirt, and here we wore a polo shirt buttoned up. The neck was itchy and uncomfortable. I was pleased not to have to wear a tie, though – at my last school I had once tied such a tight a knot in my tie that I couldn't get it out, and it took the teacher ages to undo it!

This school had smaller lessons and everything moved a bit more slowly. There were nineteen children in each class, but only a few others in the school had Down syndrome. Most people there had different levels and types of autism. The LSAs were really friendly, and there were usually two of them in each class with the teacher, so I didn't have one person who was there just for me. I could walk around the school and have lunch with my friends. There were lots of people around to make sure we were OK, but they didn't sit with us.

I was in one of the classes for children with milder learning difficulties, so we still did some tricky exercises. The classes were only an hour at my new school, which was easier to manage, but I still needed breaks every now and again. Drama was my favourite subject, and I was good at English. At this school we did PE, including cross-country running, which was my least favourite thing to do ever! There were two fields next to each other and they wanted us to do a whole lap of both. I couldn't do it. I got halfway round and just sat on the floor, panting. When I had recovered, I got up and walked the rest of the way. I need lots of stamina and energy for my job in the fashion industry now – but it's so much easier when it's something you enjoy!

I did some really fun trips with this school. They took me to see all the exotic fish at the aquarium. We also did residential holidays, where we went somewhere in Derbyshire for five days and got to try out loads of activities like caving, abseiling, wood craft and a ropes course. I felt like I was doing well, and I passed all my entry-level tests.

Mum thinks those two years were my best, and that I progressed the most there. It was definitely a calmer environment than the one before, and everything felt so much smoother, but it wasn't easy for Mum and Dad. The school was fifty minutes in the car from our house, so they could be driving for nearly three-and-a-half hours each day if they dropped me off and picked me up. Sounds exhausting, doesn't it? Usually, Mum would take me one way and Dad would do the other. They said it was worth it so I could go to the best school possible, and I did love it. The teachers there understood me better than a lot of my previous ones.[1]

At that time the school didn't have a sixth form, so I had to leave when I was sixteen. They've opened one up now, but I was a few years too early. I left with only happy memories of my time there, but sadly I couldn't say the same about my next school. Before we get to that, let's talk about Ellie's beloved grandmother for a moment.

---

1 Yvonne: They really grasped that Ellie's condition and character were two completely separate things.

18
Grandma Freda

I think about my grandma a lot. Her name was Freda, and she was my mum's mum. I'm sure I got my cheekiness from her; we were very cheeky together. Everyone said how alike we were, and I loved spending time with her.

I used to see Grandma almost every day. She lived just five minutes down the road, and Sunday mornings were our special time together. We would hang out at her house and eat bagels with salmon and cream cheese (delicious!).

A couple of times she looked after me and Amy for the whole weekend so Mum and Dad could have a little break. Those times she came to our house to stay, and it was a lot of fun. She used to love quiz shows like *The Price is Right* and *Family Fortunes*, and all the *Carry On* films. She gave us cake and biscuits, and she taught me a pat-a-cake game called tic-tac-toe. I can still remember it today!

Grandma wasn't at all strict with me – she was the best. I'm very sad she's gone. I was very upset at the time, but I understand that people eventually go to heaven. Now I just like to remember her. I think about her when we're walking through the shops and I see a striped cardigan that would have been just her style. I'll point it out to Mum and say, 'Oh, Grandma would have liked that!' It's been more than ten years now, but she's still very present in our lives.

A word from Yvonne

I am so sad that my mum isn't here to see how well Ellie's doing in the fashion industry and beyond. Something I loved about her was that she never failed to see Ellie's full potential. When everyone else told us what she couldn't do, my mum would always tell us how much Ellie was going to achieve. She always believed that Ellie could do anything – she knew her granddaughter would be a star. She said it often. Sometimes I wonder if she said it so much that the world was hypnotised into thinking it was true!

Mum was ninety-one when she passed away. She had me when she was older, and then I had Ellie when I was older, so the gap between them was big. Mum was in her eighties when Ellie was born, but despite her age she was always so active and involved in Amy and Ellie's lives. She would tell me to just drop the kids over on Sunday morning so I could have a couple of hours to myself. I think any mum can agree that when the children are young, a couple of hours of 'me time' is a godsend.

Mark and I even managed to get away for the odd weekend here and there because she would come and stay at our house for the night and watch the girls. She helped us so much, and it meant that she had a really close relationship with both of them.

She was a real soft touch when it came to both Amy and Ellie. I thought it was nice that they had someone like that in their lives. That's what grandparents are for, isn't it? Sometimes when I dropped them off at her flat I would say goodbye and then proceed to push my ear up against the door just to hear how the girls were settling in without me. All I ever heard was Mum doting on them: 'Right – what shall I get you to eat?' They would demand all kinds of sandwiches and chocolate and cake. Then she'd go off to the kitchen to fetch it for them – knowing full well that I would have said they couldn't have it if I'd been there!

She was so kind, loyal and full to the brim with character. She was outgoing and never cared what anyone else thought of her. Mum was married to my dad for fifty years, but when he died she decided not to remarry. She said, 'Why would I want to do someone else's washing?' But just because she decided to stay single, that didn't mean she lacked attention from the men. She loved a good flirt and would often have us all in stitches with her comments to the fellas. Sometimes I wonder if that's where Ellie's sassiness and confidence comes from. They spent so much time together that some of it must have rubbed off.

Things took a turn for Mum when she had a stroke in her late eighties. It happened when we were out at the shops. Everything was completely normal, and then all of a sudden she sounded really weird. I was panicked and said, 'Mum! Why are you talking like that?' Then I noticed that her face had changed. I took her arm and marched her over to Marks and Spencer, where the staff called us an ambulance.

It was there in ten minutes, and the two paramedics loaded her up into the back of the vehicle on a gurney. I got in and sat next to her, while the paramedics tended to her and ran tests. Her face and voice returned to normal during the drive, and suddenly she was her old self again. She told the paramedic how handsome he was, and I was half laughing, half horrified as I reminded her, 'Mum! You've just had a stroke!'

She recovered well, but from then on she had to take blood thinners. It wasn't long before she was up and about, doing things around the house and asking to look after the kids again. She was the strongest woman I've ever known (apart from Ellie, maybe).

Even though there was no long-term damage, something did change. It knocked us all back, and after that I think we were all conscious of how fragile and precious life was.

She was on top form at her ninetieth birthday in 2011. We threw her a surprise party at our house, and the whole family turned out to celebrate with her. The place was decked out with balloons and birthday decorations. We gave her a massive birthday cake, and everyone stood around and sang to her. She was in her element.

Her health started to deteriorate from the age of ninety-one. She had a lot of hospital visits, and I went with her to as many as I could.

When it became clear that she needed more help, I arranged for carers to go in a couple of times a day to check on her and help out with some of the day-to-day tasks. She hated it. My mum was so particular about the way she liked things to be done that she didn't want a stranger coming in to make her breakfast. She just wanted things done her way (again, very Ellie!). When she was able, the bed was made the second she got out of it, before she did anything else. I remember her saying to me, 'I've taught the carer how to make the bed the way I like it!'

Towards the end, the most upsetting thing was that she didn't look like herself any more. She was usually immaculately turned out, with her hair perfectly in place (we used to say she looked like Maggie Thatcher!). She always wore perfectly ironed blouses with big bows. I, on the other hand, would go around without brushing my hair, exhausted from the two little ones, and she would say, 'Look at the state of you!' She was always on the go and wore heels well into her eighties! But of course, she couldn't keep that going right to the end.

Ellie was ten years old when Grandma Freda died, four months away from her ninety-second birthday. She was at home. We had known the end was coming, so I'd stayed with her for a few nights beforehand so she wouldn't be alone. She didn't want to be anywhere but in her own bed. My brother and his wife flew over from their home in Barcelona to see her, and there were nurses with her, too.

With so many people suddenly around, Mark and I nipped out to quickly get some food. Not long after, my phone rang. It was my sister-in-law telling me to come straight away. We rushed back to Mum's and sat by her bedside for her last few minutes. Amy was sixteen, so she was with us, but we asked a friend to look after Ellie as we didn't want her to be too upset, and we didn't think she would understand.

One of the last things she said was, 'Where's my Ellie? Where's my Amy?' I reassured her that Ellie was fine and told her that Amy was there with us. I was touched that, even in that final moment, she was so worried about the girls and wanted to see them.

After she passed away and we collected Ellie, I told her that Grandma had gone to heaven. My mum had recorded a short video message to play for Ellie when she was older. I can't bring myself to watch it, but I know Ellie does because I've heard it coming from her room before.

Ellie didn't react well when she heard the news. I didn't know what to do. The school started calling, saying she was acting up and was more frustrated than usual. The headmistress didn't seem very sympathetic to the fact that she was grieving and was finding it hard to work through.

Grief is difficult for anyone to process, but Ellie had always tended to tuck her feelings away rather than speak about them. If you asked how she was, she was always 'fine', even if there was a lot bubbling under the surface. Ellie was used to seeing her grandma every day and, although she finds some aspects of change exciting, routine is really important to her. It was clear that Ellie was struggling, but I was too, and I couldn't see a way through it. It was a hard time, but focusing on Ellie when I had just lost my mum gave me a distraction that was probably helpful.

Amy was in her late teens at this point. She was very upset, but she had more tools to cope with her grief than Ellie. I was still worried about Amy, but she was mature for her age and understood that her grandma had been ill, so she recognised the build-up and had prepared herself in a way that Ellie couldn't. Of course, it was still a shock. Even if you're expecting someone to pass away, it doesn't stop it being a shock.

In the end we managed to get Ellie some therapy sessions through the council, so she could talk about her grandma and how she was feeling. They helped her write down stories about their time together and made a scrapbook of her favourite memories. They added photos of Ellie and Amy with Grandma Freda, including some of them all playing tic-tac-toe, a game they loved.

It took time for Ellie to start feeling OK again, and she's not good at putting words to her emotions. Instead, it showed in her behaviour. She had never experienced those emotions before and, just like a lot of us when faced with a bereavement, didn't know what to do with them. She had gone from seeing her grandmother all the time to not seeing her at all, and that was painful.

Now all we're left with are happy memories. Ellie still brings up her grandma from time to time, which is so comforting for me. I love that I can see so much of my mum in her.

19

The worst school ever

Back to Ellie

When other people moved on to sixth form, I started at my third and last secondary school. It was supposed to be for people with moderate learning difficulties, but it was probably more like moderate-to-severe. Some pupils there needed a lot more special support and care than I did. It should have been a great fit for me, but it turned out to be the worst year of my life up to that point.

They didn't really get me, and they treated me as a person with Down syndrome, not as Ellie. They thought I was naughty and disruptive, and didn't take the time to really talk to me. They didn't want me to have an opinion or be my usual chatty self. They just wanted to me to sit quietly. It seemed like they didn't care about what I cared about or what I enjoyed. They didn't even take the time to find out what my favourite subjects were. They just made me feel like a problem. I was used to being treated like any other student, as I had at the other schools, but to them I was just a person with a disability.

It was a struggle to be seen from day one. Even when Mum took me for a walk around the school and to meet the teachers, something felt strange. The headteacher came over to say hi, but before he spoke he took a step back and looked me up and down, which didn't feel very kind. Then he immediately started speaking to me in sign language. A lot of people with Down's who struggle with their speech use it, but he had assumed I couldn't speak to him normally, and he hadn't even asked me!

Mum said she didn't want me to go there but there wasn't any choice, as it was the only school where they could place me. My previous school didn't take pupils after the age of sixteen and I wasn't ready for a proper mainstream college. I think she hoped it wouldn't be as bad as we thought.

There was no terrible moment when everything went wrong; it's just that they didn't know me. I think because they knew about Down syndrome and had learned all about it, they just treated me like a person from a textbook without seeing me as an individual. It made me feel so sad. Seeing as they had other people with Down's in their school, they should have known how different we all are, but they didn't. At my previous school, they hadn't seemed to see me that way. I felt as if I could try new and fun things, and they told me when I was doing well, but in this new school I was held back.

Towards the end it all got too much for me. One day I had a panic attack in the classroom. I just started to feel like I couldn't breathe. I began coughing and gagging, trying to slow down so I could get some air. It was so unsettling. I was grateful when the year was over and I finally got to leave. I hoped much better things were ahead.

Yvonne's perspective

I really do agree with Ellie that this was the worst year of her life. So much of her education and her excitement about learning new things completely stalled, and she slipped backwards. A lot of the independence she had earned at the other schools was taken away from her again. Have you ever seen anyone you love just slowly losing their energy and their spirit? It's absolutely heartbreaking, and we felt really helpless.

They didn't bother to learn what Ellie's capabilities were before they started to teach her. I should have known that they wouldn't nurture Ellie properly after that first meeting with the headteacher. The whole thing really got my back up!

I remember at one parent's evening the teacher telling me all the things Ellie couldn't do. I got so furious that I stopped her and explained that Ellie had previously been really good at English and enjoyed it a lot. I said we knew maths wasn't her strongest subject, but she'd been progressing well in science and that she had a great memory. I knew I wasn't just being a pushy parent because every teacher she'd had before had said the same. This teacher was unimpressed and responded by reminding me that, 'There are cleverer children than Ellie here.' To be honest, I didn't care how clever the other kids were and I didn't need Ellie to be the cleverest. I was just so frustrated that she didn't see Ellie's talents and potential. Plus, I was there to speak about *my* daughter at the parents' evening – not everyone else's!

The drama teacher didn't seem to like Ellie either, which was upsetting because she loved to perform (as we all know!). Ellie was always pushed to the back of shows in favour of the teacher's go-to favourites. I knew she was good on stage; we'd already taken her to a drama club out of school, where she had achieved a London Academy of Music and Dramatic Art (LAMDA) qualification. Ellie had been singing and dancing with some success.

Despite all this, the drama teacher called me in one day to say that they were doing *Grease*, but Ellie 'can't act or remember any of her lines in the show'. I thought she was joking. I told the teacher how well Ellie was doing with her acting outside of school, and she replied with, 'What? *Her?*'

It's a good thing Grandma Freda raised me well, otherwise I would have come up with a few very special words for her in response. I was so upset by her attitude, and I just wanted to protect Ellie from anyone who said that she couldn't do things.

Jane Jessop, who founded Blue Apple Theatre for people with all sorts of physical and learning disabilities, shared with us that she really wanted people to understand that those with Down syndrome can lead active, healthy and happy lives, with their own opinions and ideas. She said people often assume people with Down's have no talent – but they really do! I found it so frustrating when people couldn't see past Ellie's Down syndrome to the variety in her character, intellect, interests and talents.

This teacher didn't think Ellie was good enough for a production of *Grease* at a school with moderate learning difficulties, so I decided it was better not to argue with her any more. There didn't seem to be much point. We had worked so hard to make sure that she had opportunities and wasn't underestimated, but it felt as if we had hit a new low. I know life is different for Ellie, but I always want her to feel encouraged.

By the end of that year, Ellie hadn't moved any further forward with her education, and they expected her to sit the same exams she had taken the year before. I asked if she could move to the next stage, as she had already passed those tests, but they said no. I guess it would have been too much work for them to offer her something different, even though we had spoken about it before Ellie enrolled. Their students sat these tests, and it didn't matter that we had already ticked the box somewhere else.

Of course, this meant that Ellie wasn't stretched. She was being taught the same things again and it was boring for her. I got a call every time something went wrong to tell me that Ellie had been badly behaved. Every time there was a new hurdle or we had another difficult conversation with the school, Mark and I would go back to our original plan of taking one day at a time. It was all we could do.

On one occasion, Ellie had said to a friend that she thought two of the students who were dating had broken up. This caused a big row between the couple, which ended up in a few punches being thrown. Ellie wasn't involved in the fight, but I was the parent who was called in because Ellie had 'started it'. I couldn't believe it. In the end I just brushed off the complaints and thought, *Roll on July, so we can get her out of here.*

The worst part for me was when she had that panic attack in class. It's horrible to think of your child feeling so upset, and not being well looked after or comforted. Towards the end of that year I got a call from the school because she had been scratching her own arms. I was distraught. Ellie was so bubbly, vibrant and full of life, and suddenly she was hurting herself. I had never seen these behaviours before, she had completely plummeted.

I spoke to Ellie immediately about the scratching and we nipped it in the bud. I asked her why she was doing it, and she explained that lots of the girls did the same, so that's where she'd got the idea. She is so visual, and I know that if she saw another student getting attention for it, she would have remembered and maybe thought it was a good way to get attention for herself. I explained that it was really important for her to look after herself, and how bad it was to scratch her arms. It often seems as if Ellie isn't listening, but she does respond and that's what she did this time. That was the last time she ever deliberately hurt herself.

I was so relieved when that year ended, and we finally got to take her out and put her into a mainstream college. Ellie's physical, mental and emotional health all seemed to have been negatively impacted there, and we knew we needed a positive change. We spoke to a clinical psychologist and the bestselling author of *Why Has Nobody Told Me This Before?*, Dr Julie Smith, who told us how closely linked our physical, mental and emotional health are.

She explained: 'Any moment in your life can be broken down into these different aspects of your experience. The thoughts going through your mind, the emotions that you feel, the physical sensations that come with that, and your behaviour. Each of these things is closely connected. They all constantly influence each other.' We could certainly see this in Ellie's case. 'In fact, they are like weaves in a basket, interacting to create our experience,' Dr Julie continued. 'But we don't always have a clear sense of the different weaves. We experience the basket as a whole. Often when we try to make a positive change in one of these, we focus in on that, neglecting the fact that it is impacted so heavily by these other areas.'

Looking back, we can see how being at an ill-fitting school impacted the entirety of our wonderful daughter. We hoped for better days ahead, but none of us could have known what would happen next or how it would impact our lives.

20
College girl

Ellie again...

I started college in 2020, studying Performing Arts, and I absolutely love it. In September 2023 I'll start my Level 3 extended certificate, finishing in July 2024. I got distinctions in all my previous exams, so I'm hoping for the same this year.

My college is really big, but I don't struggle to find my way around as much now because most of my classes are in the theatre and the studio, which are in a separate building from the rest of the college. I still have to go to class in the main building four times a week for two maths lessons (urgh!) and two English lessons.

College feels totally different from school. When I walk in past the security guards each morning they all know me and say, 'Hi darling!' I know so many of the teachers and staff, as I've been there for four years now. Being at college is such a big part of my life.

I have an LSA at college, too. Her name's Nasima and she's a bit firm – although Mum says I need it.[1] She's really kind and we get on well; I think she just wants the best for me. She makes me work hard in maths and English – but then I did pass both my tests with eighty per cent this year, so maybe it's worth it (only maybe!). Lunchtime is great. I sit with my friends and we have a good catch-up.

There are lots of things I like about college – like how I only go for four days a week, so I get Fridays at home. Three-day weekends are the best! I also really love my English teacher. Aly my drama teacher and Lydia my dance teacher are the best. They have supported me in every way, and love seeing me in my campaigns and watching where my career is taking me. They are just fab. It's so wonderful to know how much the staff at college believe in me. They've helped me come a long way in my studies.

---

1   Yvonne: Otherwise, Ellie would run rings around her!

In drama we are always putting on different plays. We spend the whole term rehearsing and then do a big performance at the end. Our performances count towards our final assessments, so its important for me to enjoy it, but also to work hard.

My favourite production was *The Twisted Side of Oz*, which was a new take on *The Wizard of Oz*. I played a munchkin and a jitterbug, and both were in the dancing chorus. At the very end I had to crawl around on the floor. It was very different from the normal *Wizard of Oz*, where Dorothy follows the yellow-brick road to find the wizard. In our version there were two Dorothys – one in each act – and one of them was in a mental asylum. It was quite dark, but very exciting! I was in so many songs and dances, I just loved it.

In June 2023 we did *Heathers: The Musical*, which my teachers adapted slightly. We rehearsed so much, it was really hard work. I was given the job of being dance captain and also a rock chick. The songs and dances were amazing to perform, and the play was so much fun. I really enjoyed being part of it and performing to big audiences four times.

I've loved drama since I was eight, when my mum first took me to Redbridge Drama Centre on Saturday mornings. We played fun games, did warm-ups and rehearsed for performances. The first show I remember being in was *The Nutcracker*, and I once did a whole solo of 'Let It Go' from *Frozen*. Mum said she could see that I had a flair for acting because I like to be the centre of attention!

I'm lucky, as I can learn and memorise lines really quickly. I think it's because I'm such a good reader and love books so much. When I was thirteen I attended another drama group called Raw. We did some really good shows, but I think my passion is more towards dancing. I love performing on stage.

When we spoke to Jane Jessop from Blue Apple Theatre, she said that the people with learning difficulties who join her classes find it gives them the freedom to express themselves, as well as interesting and exciting things to talk about. Plus, learning lines and dance routines, and working together to create something beautiful, is good for their mental health. She said it also gives them safe friendships and a sense of belonging, and I totally agree. I love being part of a show with my friends and entertaining an audience.

21

Dancing queen

I was five years old when I properly discovered dancing, but my mum says I was bobbing around to music before I could walk. Every time any music came on the telly or the radio I would jiggle about to the beat, so Mum signed me up for a lunchtime club. Once a week I would go off with Miss Shosh and learn a routine. I was only five and it was very simple, but I loved it instantly. I danced about to Kesha's 'TiK ToK' like I didn't have a care in the world. Because I didn't!

Miss Shosh set up an after-school class, so I joined that. I kept dancing there for a while, but eventually she had to stop running the sessions, so I moved to another dance school. I didn't love it as much. I could pick up the routines and loved to move and jump about to the music, but the group didn't have the same welcoming atmosphere. Mum would get frustrated when she came to shows and performances because I'd always be tucked away at the back. Eventually they said I could only join in the classes if someone came with me to keep an eye on me. It was hard to hear. I knew I was cheeky, but I was never really badly behaved.

The teacher probably thought it was her lucky day when my mum called in to say that I couldn't come to the classes any more. It wasn't because of the lessons or because I wasn't given the opportunity to dance at the front of the stage during performances; it was because I broke my ankle. I was fifteen at the time, and it was just a normal weekend. We had headed out to the park with our dog, Poppy. I was wearing trainers, jeans and a jumper, as I usually did, but it had been raining, so the ground was really wet. We walked over the grass and through the trees, playing and exploring the park.

I went to pet Poppy but she thought we were playing, so she ran away. She started running straight down a grassy hill. I heard Mum shout for me to stop, but I was already focused and just wanted to catch up with her, so I kept running. I sped up down the hill, running as fast as I could, but then I felt my foot get caught. It turned under my body till it was folded backwards, and I put my weight down on my ankle. I fell to the ground in pain as Poppy continued to run off. Mum came rushing over to check on me while I held my leg and foot. It was so painful, but I try never to show when I'm hurt. I couldn't hide it this time, though. I couldn't help but cry.

Mum picked me up and took a look at my ankle, which was already bruised and starting to swell. I had to hop all the way back to the car, resting on Mum's shoulder, because it hurt too much to put pressure on my leg. By the time we got back it had swollen as if someone had blown up a balloon inside my foot. It looked awful.

We went to hospital, but they said it would calm down and to let it heal naturally. They didn't want to operate because of my heart condition, so they put me in a plaster cast, which was very itchy and uncomfortable. They gave me a wheelchair because I wasn't able to walk well with crutches. The plaster cast went right up over my knee and onto my thigh, and I had it on for three whole months.

It was hard to move around, and I had to sit in the shower with a bag over my cast so it wouldn't get wet. I had to go up the stairs at home on my bum, bouncing up one step at a time. When I got to the top of the stairs, I had to swing my leg over the banister to get into the hallway that led to my room. It's a good thing I've always been flexible or I would have been stuck! I took it in my stride, but I was really sad when I found out I wouldn't be able to dance for a whole year. I cried a lot when they told me that.

After three months they took off the cast, and I could finally scratch my leg. It felt so funny having it out of that horrible cast and feeling the air on my skin. They gave me a chunky boot to keep my leg and ankle safe, but I quite liked wearing it. Mum and Dad were still worried, so they took me back to Great Ormond Street, where I'd had my heart operation as a baby. They spoke to another set of doctors who did an X-ray and said that it should have been operated on at the time. They said the two bits of bone should have been pinned so they would fuse together, but they had just healed separately and never reconnected. By then, it was too late to join them up.

When the boot came off I got an ankle strap and they made me do some physiotherapy. The leg that had been in the cast was really skinny compared to the other one because I hadn't been using it. I'd lost all my muscle and it looked really strange. A physio took me along to a little gym and made me do all sorts of exercises. I had to move my leg around and jog on a treadmill. It took six sessions before I got some strength back and could use my leg normally again. My leg is much better now, but it's not back to how it was. Sometimes even now when I'm dancing or moving around it'll feel creaky, or I'll feel it click or even swell up, which reminds me that I hurt myself. I think the doctors did what they thought what was best, though. It's hard for them to always know the right thing to do.

As soon as I was allowed, I went back to my dance classes and carried on improving. I can now do the splits both ways, put my legs behind my head and do a round-off cartwheel (a cartwheel where you land on both feet together). I feature in dance shows all the time with my current school, Straight Up Dance. Before Christmas we do a panto, and for the panto in 2022 we danced to loads of different songs. We did 'Umbrella' by Rhianna, 'Birthday' by Ann Marie, 'Toxic' by Britney Spears and loads more.

There was a different outfit for every song and only a short time to change. Once in rehearsals I took so long to get out of my bright-pink outfit for 'Toxic' that I missed the start of the next number! Thank goodness I didn't do that in the real performance. We did eight shows in two weekends, which is totally exhausting, but I loved it! I wish I could do a dance show every weekend.

It wasn't just the broken ankle that could have stopped me from dancing, though. As Mum explained earlier, I had a very serious operation on my heart when I was a baby. At one point I was starting to feel out of breath during the warm-ups for my dance class. I had been all right before, but suddenly I was getting really tired. I felt a burning and a bumping in my chest while I was running around.

I knew it couldn't be right, but I was nervous to tell anyone. I don't like to say when I'm not well because I don't want to make a fuss, but I did tell my dance teacher in the end.

I went for a check-up, but I'd missed the previous two years of appointments because of Covid. Apparently, doctors can never completely repair a heart valve, so there's always a little bit of leaking, but this time the leakage had increased and they said my condition was 'moderate to severe'.

They needed to monitor me some more, so they hooked me up to a heart monitor, which I had to wear for a while. I don't like having stickers and tubes on my chest; it means I can't do cartwheels. I also had to have some blood tests, which I don't like either. The results came back, and the doctors were happy that there was nothing too serious, so I could carry on dancing. Phew! I'm pleased they weren't too worried, but they still want to keep a close eye on my heart, and I have to tell them straight away if I have any problems.

There was one bonus that came out of it all. Before I had the heart check-up, I had to start the dance class with ten laps, fifteen burpees, a one-minute plank, push-ups and tricycle crunches – which was a lot of work! Now I just do my power walking as a warm-up instead. It's way better. The doctors said how good it is that I dance, because it's such great exercise and I enjoy it. It's really good for me.

If you've never danced, I really think you'd love it – especially with the right songs. If you're too scared to try it, or you're worried it'll be embarrassing while you're a beginner, my advice is to just twerk it out! Be confident and be happy. I'm never nervous about dancing, and you shouldn't be either. It doesn't matter what other people think – just be you. Enjoy yourself and go for it!

22

Now That's What I Call... Ellie's favourite songs to dance to

Dancing always makes me feel happy, but you need the right songs to help you feel the rhythm, so make a playlist of all the best upbeat music you love. Sometimes on down days – particularly the ones where you feel sluggish and lack motivation – it can really help to listen to some music and move your body. It doesn't have to be dancing; sometimes just going for a walk around the block with your headphones on can help. Why not make a different playlist for different activities or moods? If you can't think of any songs that pick you up and make you feel happy right now, you can borrow some of mine!

'Undecided' by Chris Brown
'When I Grow Up' by the Pussycat Dolls
'Hollaback Girl' by Gwen Stefani
'The Room Where It Happens' from the musical *Hamilton*
'Wow.' by Post Malone
'Circus' by Britney Spears
'Finesse' by Bruno Mars
'A Million Dreams' from the musical *The Greatest Showman*
'From Now On' also from *The Greatest Showman*
'Out Out' by Joel Corry and Jax Jones, featuring Charli XCX and Saweetie

23

Ellie's Moves

A word from Beca Barnard (Straight Up Dance and Theatre School)

I first met the cheeky madam that is Ellie Goldstein back in August 2017, when Ellie came along to my summer dance camp. The lovely Yvonne rang me before they showed up to explain that Ellie had Down syndrome and to ask if I would be happy for her join the sessions. I had never taught anyone with Down's before, so we had a long conversation about what Ellie would need, and I was keen for her to come and dance with us. We agreed that Yvonne wouldn't be too far away at first, just in case we had any issues and I needed to give her a call.

I had no clue what Ellie would be capable of doing on the dance floor or what she would be like – I'd never met anyone like her before. But to be honest, you'll never meet anyone else like Ellie. She truly is one of a kind.

I tried to keep an open mind and not to expect anything from her – either good or bad. I just wanted to get to know her and see what she could do. Ellie threw herself into the dances and blew me away with her energy and talent. We practised a number of routines, all to chart music, and I was surprised at how quickly she picked up the choreography. She was never afraid to ask questions if something wasn't clear to her. And the girl can really move!

When the summer camp ended, Ellie kept coming to the dance and theatre school for after-school classes and weekend sessions. She is at exactly the same level as the other girls who have been learning for the same amount of time. She never lets anything hold her back. Not only that, but she's so dedicated. She would leave our classes and send me videos of herself practising the routines that same evening.

I loved seeing Ellie fit in with the other girls in the class, and now we've got an incredible squad. She's part of the gang – and a real joker. Sometimes she'll wait for a silence when I'm changing the music and then let out a loud fart to make everyone laugh! Everyone is beside themselves with laughter. She's very clever and her comedic timing is always perfect. She knows exactly what she's doing to keep people entertained.

Ellie is fearless. When I started as a dancer, it was intimidating. I used to show up at London's famous Pineapple Dance Studios and it was scary. Going to any new class is. I recently had a friend who really wanted to come to some of my sessions but was terrified that he would be rubbish. When the time for his class came he almost didn't show up, but he eventually got inside the room and now he's so pleased he did. Ellie really models that bravery for me and for others. She always turns up. I think she's really confirmed for me that hard work pays off, and that no one should ever be excluded from dancing. You're never too old, young or incapable. You only live once and you have to try new things – even if it means being a beginner for a while.

We can all learn from the way Ellie throws herself into new things. She ignores the rules and what society says about her and others. There is no stopping her, and I love to watch her go. I have people contacting me all the time because they want to meet and dance with her. One person even messaged me to ask her out on a date! I can see why people gravitate towards her – she's an inspiration. And I'm sure she's only just getting started.

24

Model behaviour

More from Ellie

My modelling career started because my mum's friend was watching daytime TV one day. It was a normal day, so I was at school. Mum got a call from her friend Emma, who said she had been watching *Good Morning Britain* and they'd had these women on the show talking about their modelling agency. She told Mum they had models who looked different, and that they seemed like really nice people. She said we should try to speak to them.

The agency was called Zebedee. Mum searched for them online and liked the look of their website, so she gave them a ring. She told them all about me. I'm not sure what she said, but it worked – because they asked us to meet them in London for a trial photo shoot.

They came all the way from Sheffield, and there were plenty of other people at the East London studio where we met them. When it was my turn, I had to take pictures in a few different outfits and they took videos, too. I wore a cute denim dress and a checked top; my favourite things from my wardrobe. I didn't feel nervous. I just did my best poses and chatted to everyone. The photographer made the whole shoot fun and I felt at home.

They asked me a few questions, such as my name and my age, and we had a little chat, but it wasn't very intense. Mum told me that while I was posing for my photos one of the ladies who ran the agency told her I'd be very good at modelling – and that I was a livewire!

The trial shoot went really well. We both loved the day out, so I was really excited when I heard that Zebedee wanted to sign me and I would be one of their models. I couldn't believe it! I didn't want to get too excited, but I loved the idea of being on the cover of a magazine or wearing a fashion designer's clothes. I imagined photo shoots with hair and make-up assistants and lots of glamorous pictures. Of course, plenty of models get signed up to an agency but don't manage to get jobs, so I knew I had to wait and see what would happen, and that I shouldn't get ahead of myself.

As predicted, nothing happened for ages. The agency photo shoot was in November 2016, but we didn't hear much in December because everyone was busy with Christmas. It took a while for everything to get sorted so that I would show up on their website. That meant even though I was 'on their books' – that's what they say when they sign a new model – I wasn't actually ready for auditions until February or March 2017. Even then, we still had to wait months for anyone to want to meet us. It wasn't until July that we got our first call… but it was a big one.

Zebedee called mum to tell her that Superdrug wanted to meet me. Superdrug! I'd been into Superdrug loads – there was one on our high street. And now they wanted to see me! And even more exciting than that… it was to audition for their Christmas advert. It was only July, but they were getting everything ready, and the Christmas advert was to be their biggest of the year.

We got the email through with the time and place of the audition. I still didn't feel nervous. I think Mum was more worried about it than I was. I just wanted to meet them straight away to show them my dancing and my poses.

I was so excited when the day finally came for us to go to London. We got the tube all the way to Oxford Street, then walked to the place where Superdrug had told us to meet them. It was on a road called East Castle Street, and when we got there we went through the main door and walked up some stairs. At the top there was a room where lots of people were waiting to audition. It was so busy. I think there were 100 people there.[1] Everyone was just

---

1 Yvonne: It was more like sixty, but it did feel really busy!

standing around or sitting on the floor. It was quite squashed, but we found a spot and waited.

There was one other girl there with Down syndrome, but there were people from all different age groups, abilities, and shapes and sizes. When working on this book, we spoke with international fashion director and journalist Zadrian Smith about the power of having a diverse range of people represented within the fashion industry. He can still recall the day that he first saw the first black, transgender and physically disabled model Aaron Rose Philip emerging onto the scene. Aaron was represented by a modelling agency and was the face of Moschino's autumn–winter 2020 collection. She also debuted exclusively for the spring–summer 2022 Moschino show.

'She has not only pushed the industry forward in terms of inclusivity, but continues to pursue change fearlessly,' Zadrian told us. 'I say fearlessly, because when you try to create change the naysayers can infiltrate, and to rise above that for the bigger cause is not an easy feat.

'To me, seeing models like [Aaron Rose] Philip break the boundaries represents hope; hope that change is coming, whether the industry is ready or not. I admire their tenacity and motivation to continue to push, despite the barriers that the industry continues to raise, and I know that it will inspire people to see that there are no boundaries.'

It was so wonderful to see people of different shapes and sizes walk into the Superdrug shoot as they called one person into the audition room at a time. I think they probably had hundreds of people come in to see them! We waited for two hours in the end, and then someone opened the door to the audition room and said my name. I jumped up to go in. I had waited so long – I just wanted to get in there.

I left Mum waiting outside and walked into the room. It wasn't very big, and there were just two people in there, sitting behind a table. They each had an open laptop in front of them. They were friendly and seemed happy to meet me. They asked me for my name, so I introduced myself and we had a quick chat. Then they said they wanted me to dance to 'Bang Bang' by Jessie J, Ariana Grande and Nicki Minaj. They turned on the music and I started dancing. I didn't have a routine ready, so I just freestyled. I whipped my long hair around and kicked my legs in time to the 'bang bang' bit in the chorus. It was a lot of fun.

As I left, the women were super kind and said 'Well done' for the audition. I said goodbye and went out to tell Mum how it had gone. We got the tube home and waited to hear back.

We didn't have to wait long, because the next day Zebedee called Mum to say that the Superdrug people wanted to meet me again! Mum said this was a good sign. We went back to the exact same place on the tube. This time it was nowhere near as busy as before. I didn't recognise anyone from the first time we were there, and everything felt a lot calmer. We waited again, but not for as long.

At my first audition I had danced for the people from the advertising company, but this time the Superdrug team wanted to see me as well. I went into the same room and everything looked just like before, with two people sitting in front of computers. They had a camera hooked up to a TV screen in another room where everyone from Superdrug could watch my audition. They let Mum look through the window into the Superdrug room so she could see me dancing on the telly.

There were a lot of people watching, but it didn't put me off. When they turned Jessie J on this time, I danced even harder. I put my arms up in the air and moved my feet and spun around. I did the same hair-swinging and leg-kicking moves. I even added in some twerking this time. I enjoyed it so much!

I left feeling so happy that I had been able to dance again, even though we didn't know if I would be in the advert. I felt confident that I would be, but Mum said that you never know, so we had to wait until we heard back from them.

Two days later we were all at home when Mum's mobile phone rang. It was one of the agents from Zebedee and she just said, 'She got it!' Mum looked up at me and said, 'You got the Superdrug advert!' We both screamed. It was so exciting I couldn't contain myself. It was the best news ever. I was going to be on TV – in a Christmas advert for Superdrug!

The whole job was like a dream come true. I felt like a pampered princess. It all started a few days before the shoot, when they sent a posh car to take me from my house in Essex into London to get my nails done. We went to a fancy salon, where they gave me a full manicure, filed my nails and put cream on my hands to make the skin all soft. I didn't get to choose the colour because Superdrug knew which ones they wanted in the advert. Mine were a sparkly silver colour that looked glittery every time I moved my fingers. They were so Christmassy – even though it was August!

The next day they sent another car to take me back into London so I could meet with a stylist who chose the clothes I would wear for the filming. I tried on a lot of stuff, but she finally picked out two outfits for me – both big fluffy coats. In the end I filmed in a huge pink one that came up around my face and tickled my neck.

The best day of all was the filming. I got in yet another car that had been sent to take me to the studio where we were recording. That was five times I'd done that trip! I love modelling, but I never knew I would spend so much time driving to London.

It was a long day, but I felt like a star. There was even a cooked breakfast waiting for when I arrived in the morning, and then a hot lunch and dinner. The food was delicious! They put me in a chair in front of a big mirror and a make-up artist started working on my face. Someone else brushed my hair and styled it. Because it was a sparkling Christmas campaign, they put a lot of glitter in my hair. It took all day to get ready and then film all the different shots they needed. I had to do some things over and over again, so that the look was just right. But I loved it!

When we were done, Mum managed to get some of the glitter out of my hair before we went home, but it was impossible to get it all out. We got home so late that I just flopped down onto my bed and fell asleep. When I woke up there were sparkly bits all over my pillow and it went everywhere – but at least it was a reminder that my dream day had actually been real. Mum had to help me wash

1 Ellie at home, just a few weeks old.

2 Ellie (5 months) and sister Amy (7)
before Ellie's heart operation.

3 Amy (10) and Ellie (2).

4 Grandma Freda (83) and Ellie (3).

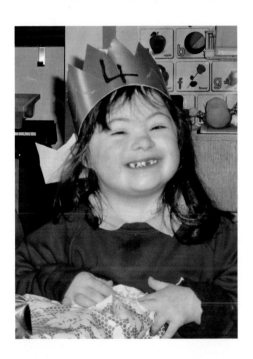

5 Ellie (4) at her nursery birthday party.

6 Ellie (7), off to a party.

7 Ellie (9) in fancy dress.

8 Ellie (20) and Beca at dance
school Straight Up Dance.

9 Ellie with her dad, Mark,
and her mum, Yvonne.

10 Ellie posing for an adidas photo shoot.

11 Ellie proudly holding the first ever Barbie Fashionistas Doll with Down Syndrome.

12 Ellie for *Noctis* magazine.

13 Amy (27) and Ellie (19).

it out, and even then we kept finding bits of glitter everywhere for days!

I know it was very lucky that I got the first job I went for, and that it doesn't happen for most models. But since then there have been lots of auditions I didn't get, and sometimes I'll be told to keep a day free because someone might want me and then they don't in the end. I never let it get me down. I think Mum gets more upset about some of the jobs I don't get than I do! Even though there are rejections, I don't mind because I know this is what I want to do, and I feel like I was born to do it. I love having fun on camera and showing the world who I am. It's the best job ever.

I don't know if you really love something – a job, a hobby or a pastime – that comes with a risk of rejection. If you do, I'd say it's worth it. There's a wise affirmation in Katie Piper's book *A Little Bit of Faith* that says: 'Nothing is a failure; it's a rehearsal.' As a performer, I really like that. But even if you can't see the positives in a rejection or a failure right now, that's OK. It's just a normal part of life. It's not about how you fall; it's about how you get back up again.

25

Call my agent

Insights from Zoe (founder of Zebedee)

I'm Zoe Proctor, and I founded Zebedee – the inclusive talent agency that signed up the wonderful Ellie. We instantly knew that Ellie had the perfect personality for modelling; she's a total firecracker! She came to one of our first casting events when we started the agency. She was fifteen years old and bursting with energy – she lit up the room!

The first thing she did when we put her in front of the camera for a screen test was do the splits! We couldn't believe how full of beans she was. It's hard not to fall in love with Ellie, and we were instantly head over heels. It was clear she had great potential. We knew we wanted to sign her to our books, but at that point we didn't know if we could actually get her any work. In the early days we didn't know if our inclusive modelling agency would actually work. In an industry famous for having people look a very specific (and unobtainable) way, we weren't sure if people would embrace our diversity message. We were careful to explain that nothing was certain, and to manage Ellie's expectations as much as possible. But when it came to the brands and casting agents, we fought tirelessly to see if we could start a shift in motion.

If you haven't taken the time to get to know someone with a disability, it's easy to assume they can't do anything. But we know that's so far from the case. We assume our models can do everything and ask them to let us know if there are any tasks that pose a challenge. As far as we're concerned, if they're capable of doing the job we'll put them forward for it – regardless of disability or learning difficulties. Even though diversity has been the focus in many industries for a little while, diversity in terms of people with disabilities has often slipped through the cracks. People don't have it in their minds that this is a group of people that needs including. We're trying to help brands become more open to working with a wider variety of people. We have a 'no silly questions' policy, so if there's anything anyone is unsure of they can just ask!

We've never had any problems with Ellie. Every single brand that has booked her has loved her as much as we do. It's her personality that makes her a great model. Her spark of mischief and huge heart come across effortlessly, and she's excellent at switching into work mode. Ellie has been pivotal in helping to change the way people with Down syndrome are perceived.

At Zebedee we just hope the work keeps coming in for our huge range of inclusive models. People don't realise that twenty per cent of people have some kind of disability, but representation in the fashion industry is nowhere near that figure. Our long-term goal is to see those numbers marry up. We would love all campaigns and shows to feature people with a disability or visible difference.

When it comes to Ellie, there is a lot more advocacy work in her future. She'll keep working with more amazing big-name brands, I'm sure of that. And I'm excited to see her continue to smash people's expectations of what a person with Down syndrome can do. I'd love to see her walk the runway at London Fashion Week!

26

Lockdown life

Back to Ellie

Modelling was a dream come true, and I was happy with my routine of college and dance classes – and then Covid hit. Like lots of people during the first UK lockdown at the start of 2020, I actually really enjoyed spending more time at home. As I was vulnerable and needed care support, Amy (who had left home by then) was able to join our household and come over to help me and Mum, so we still got to spend time with her. College was cancelled, so I didn't have to sit through my normal maths classes. That felt like a big win for me! But I was sad about the other subjects I was missing and about not seeing my college friends.

I struggled with the online teaching and found it really difficult to concentrate when I was looking at a screen the whole time. I know lots of other people felt the same way. My support worker would log in with me, and she would send me work via the chat function in Microsoft Teams. Sometimes I got so frustrated that I would slam down the lid of the laptop and want to give up for the day. When I was at college in person, I would have someone sitting with me in class, talking me through things and helping me with the exercises. It didn't work like that in Covid, so I started to feel really down. There was a lot of pressure to keep working and doing well, even when it felt very difficult. For the drama classes we were given research tasks instead of acting and performing – which was fine, but not at all the same. As a class group we did one conference call a week but also had some one-on-one time with the teachers, and I looked forward to both of those chats.

I kept at my dance classes with Beca on a Wednesday evening. I didn't mind that they were on a screen, even though they would have been better in the studio. She was brilliant at keeping our spirits up and getting us moving. We learned full dance routines, and I would practise them in my bedroom after the Zoom was over. I did some baking with Mum, and we hung out in the garden.

The second lockdown was a bit harder. I started to feel anxious, as it wasn't clear how long it would last, and I didn't want to stop going out again. I remember having a cry when they announced that we would have to stay home, but I still managed to keep the faith.

27

Loving life

People are always so interested in other people's love lives, aren't they? Well, I can't blame them. I love *love*, too. I can see why shows like *First Dates* and *The Undateables* are so popular, even though I don't watch them myself. Lots of people with Down syndrome date, and some get married – for example Down's activist Heidi Crowder, who married her husband (who also has Down syndrome) in 2020.

People who know me aren't at all surprised to know that I date. Mum calls me a man-eater! Dating is so much fun. I've had loads of boyfriends, most of whom I met at school. I think probably between ten and twenty, but I can't remember them all. The only names I remember are Jermaine, Troy, Harrison, Glen, Antony and Jack.

I started seeing my first boyfriend when I was sixteen. We met at the school for people with moderate learning difficulties (the one I didn't like – so I guess there was an upside after all). His name was Jermaine, and he was very kind. He didn't have Down's, but he had some other struggles. I don't know exactly what they were, but his learning difficulties were very mild. And he was handsome. He was a year older than me – an older man! It looked very funny when we were together, though, because I'm four foot nine and he was six foot, so there was a big height difference.

It all started in one of our classes. We should have been concentrating on the lesson, but instead he put his hand on my hand while the teacher wasn't looking. There was no way I could focus on the lesson after that! We carried on talking, and the teacher even told us off for chatting to each other so much. I knew I fancied him, and when he touched my hand I knew he fancied me, too. We were flirting with each other for a bit – I'm very good at flirting. Then I decided to be direct and ask him the question: 'Do you want to be my boyfriend?'

He said yes, and we dated for eight months. It was so much fun. He was the first person I kissed, and he kissed me a lot. He would call me after school. When February came around, he got me a very special Valentine's Day present: a gold bangle with a few bits of silver and diamantes on it. He had asked what colour bracelet I would like a few weeks before, and he got it just right. I loved it, and I still have it in my jewellery box today.

We did all sorts of things on our dates. We went for a pub lunch, walked in the park and sometimes went to the ice-cream parlour. Mum always came with us, and so did Jermaine's mum. She was very nice and she liked to keep an eye on him, just as my mum likes to be nearby for me. They didn't sit at our table or walk with us, but they stayed close by to make sure everything was OK.

In the end, Jermaine dumped me to be with another girl. He was going through a difficult time with some family stuff, and it affected him quite badly. I'm not annoyed with him and don't blame him at all. It felt like the right time for the relationship to end. When he told me, I just said, 'OK. So long, Jermaine!' and we went our separate ways. If I'm honest I think I was happy, but I still really like him as a friend.

Next I started dating Harrison. He was at the same moderate needs school, and was my favourite of all my boyfriends. Harrison was in my drama class, and we would often flirt while we were practising for the performances. He was very funny and fun to be around. He was much shorter than Jermaine. I used to joke that he was small, even though he was still taller than me! He wore glasses, and he had Down syndrome like me.

We dated for six months, and even said that we loved each other. Sometimes we would sit together and watch each other's videos on YouTube. He was an actor and had starred in *Dr Who*. It was fun to date someone who was in the media, too. He understood how great (and sometimes tiring) it could be. We had both been treated really well in our careers, but it isn't the same for everyone with

Down syndrome, which makes me feel sad. I was all right when we broke up – I try not to get too upset about these things. And I'm still proud of him for breaking down stereotypes and showing people what an incredible actor he is. And that people with visible differences deserve to be *seen*.

I was recently speaking to someone who was a little older than me. We met at a Christmas party and hit it off. We spoke on the phone for hours. I liked him, but he drove me a little bit up the wall. I brought out my best flirting techniques with him. I called him my Prince Charming and my Golden Delicious. My mum says I must have had his head spinning!

I don't have a boyfriend at the moment, but several boys are texting me. Dating is fun, but it's also fun to be free and single. I'm going to wait until I meet someone really special to date next time. I hope that, whether you're single, dating or have a partner, you don't settle for anyone who isn't really special to you.

28

Ellie's top flirting tips

Don't blame me if my tactics don't work… but I would say that you should propose to the person you love.

That won't scare them away.

Smile and then propose.

Then you can kiss them and have kids one day.

29
The call from Gucci

After the Superdrug advert, it felt like I was getting calls for auditions all the time. I felt like a real model; like modelling was my actual job. I did a River Island photo shoot for social media. I also did some filming for the game *Just Dance*, although I didn't end up being included in the final advert. The next really exciting thing that happened was with Nike.

We got a call from Zebedee saying that Nike wanted me to audition for their 2019 Women's World Cup advert. I went and tried out for it, and they liked me enough to give me the job. This one wasn't just modelling; it was acting, too. They made me celebrate like someone had just scored a goal. The director had a lot of energy and helped me to get pumped up. I imagined I was watching the World Cup Final and the lionesses had just scored the winning goal. I didn't know then that the England women's team would actually do that in the Euros three years later, encouraging little girls everywhere that they can do anything. I mustered up all my excitement, and screamed and shouted as if I'd seen them score.

The advert ran for the whole summer that year, and I started seeing my face, along with other celebrating fans, on the sides of buses, on websites and on posters. The picture was even up on those massive screens in Piccadilly Circus – so many different faces watching the football, and one of them was mine! Seeing myself up on that huge screen was like a dream, I felt so excited. Before that I was just enjoying going to the studio and doing some filming, but suddenly it all felt much more real. We do the photos and filming so far in advance that I love it when I finally see my work out in the world.

The amazing news just kept coming, and I was cast in a dance group to perform at the Royal Opera House in London. It was all arranged by Culture Device, a company that arranges 'social–cultural events' in the UK. They work with young performers with Down syndrome and I couldn't believe it when I found out they wanted me to be part of their show.

It was all ballet and contemporary dance – which is different from the usual street dance and pop songs we do at my local club. It felt very fancy and artsy. The whole show was run by a man called Daniel Vais, who's a choreographer and creative director. He taught us some new techniques, but also encouraged us to improvise. We performed our own version of 'The Rite of Spring' by Stravinsky. There was a show every Friday for three months at the Royal Opera House. The building was beautiful, with massive red curtains and the walls painted gold. Again, it was like a dream. I couldn't believe I was dancing on that stage. The final performance was in June 2019, and each week there were different people who came to see us. The audience was made up of people who had been specially invited, and sometimes that included photographers, or other dancers or people who made their own shows.

A photographer called Natalia Evelyn Bencicova (Evelyn) attended one of the performances. She came backstage before we went on, and she took my picture, as well as portraits of the other cast members. People took photos of us all the time during the show, so I didn't think anything of it. It was always fun to pose for a photographer. In the photo I was wearing my performance clothes: a cream-coloured baggy dress, a bit like a sack, with an orange stripe around the collar. I was looking up and smiling. It wasn't very glamourous, and I didn't have a lot of make-up on. My hair was just down and tucked behind my shoulders. Mum says it's a bit of a weird picture, but I liked it.

Evelyn published the photograph, and it managed to capture people's imaginations. The picture won the Taylor Wessing Photographic Portrait Prize, which meant it was on show at the National Portrait Gallery from December 2019 to February 2020. Can you imagine? Me! Ellie from Essex, who doctors said wouldn't walk or talk! I had to pinch myself. It was weird to think that people would be going to the famous gallery and looking around at the paintings and pictures, and then there would be my face. It almost felt like someone had made a mistake. But that was just the start of the wild and unexpected ride that would follow.

I never imagined that, sometime later, this photo would lead to me being scouted through a social media programme launched by Gucci Beauty in partnership with *Vogue Italia*! My photo was soon shown to the people at *Vogue Italia*, and its senior editor, Alessia Glaviano, posted it to Instagram as her picture of the day. Little did I know then that Alessia would later be working with the creative director at Gucci, Alessandro Michele – together with an entire team – to showcase me as a model; as an authentic person a diverse range of people could relate to, using make-up to tell my story of freedom in my own way.

At the time, *Vogue Italia* was working with Gucci to help the brand advertise a new mascara from their make-up collection. The scout picked 5,000 people who they thought could be in the adverts, and I was one the models they suggested. Gucci got in touch with Zebedee and said they were considering me, so we got an email from my agents telling us I was in the running. I couldn't believe that I was even in with a chance of being featured in a Gucci campaign.

It wasn't like the other jobs I'd been put up for. There was no casting, so I didn't have to show up and meet anyone in person. They just had people's pictures and went away to decide who they wanted.

A couple of weeks later we were in town when Mum got a phone call. She left the cafe and stood outside to answer it. It was Laura from Zebedee, and she said, 'Ellie's just got a job with Gucci!' Mum couldn't believe it. She rushed back in and told me, and I just said 'Oh!'

I think it took me a while to really understand how special it was. At first it was a lot to process, and I was a bit overwhelmed. The whole thing was like a big whirlwind. We called Amy to tell her, and she screamed down the phone – she was the most excited of all of us!

The day of the shoot came around and I went off to a studio in Wimbledon. Mum came with me, and I met the whole team who were there to help – my 'glam squad' for the day. The photographer was a big deal, too. His name was David PD Hyde and he's a British artist who likes to work with ethical and sustainable clothing brands. I hadn't met him before, but I liked him a lot. It was the first time I'd met the hairdresser and make-up artist as well, although I have worked with them a few times now.

The Gucci stylist had set up a rail that was bulging with clothes, and I got to try on lots of beautiful and expensive outfits. There were two other models in the campaign: a French man called Jahmal John Baptiste and a plus-size model called Enam Asiama. We all got on really well. It was just the three of us having our pictures taken. We did lots separately and then some photos together as well. The whole shoot took three days, but it was far calmer and more peaceful than I was used to from other jobs. Everyone was relaxed and there was no pressure on the models.

I loved looking at all the clothes, and I tried on every pair of sunglasses. I wasn't allowed to wear them for the photographs, though, because we were supposed to be advertising the mascara! I tried on loads of different clothes, but in the end the stylist decided on two outfits. The first had crystals all over it and the famous Gucci print with one 'G' the right way up and another upside-down. It was a see-through top with a yellowy tint and some see-through trousers. I wore a peach slip dress underneath, so I was all covered up. When we first saw it, it looked tiny. Mum told them there was no way it would fit me, but it was very stretchy, so it turned out to be the right size. I liked it; it was glamourous.

My hair was very simple. They straightened it and put in a centre parting. The make-up artist made my face look very natural. I had rosy cheeks, a little bit of gloss on my lips and the special new Gucci mascara. It was called Mascara L'Obscur and I felt fabulous wearing it. Everything was so luxurious.

The second outfit was different. It was a black dress with a high neck. The neck was a bit itchy, but I loved the dress. It had a white panel at the top with gorgeous big blue gems all around it. The sleeves were long, but they were black mesh and see-through. The glam squad kept my hair and make-up the same, classy and simple.

Lunch on set was brilliant. They asked us what we wanted from Waitrose and then someone went out to buy it. I had the best chicken mayo sandwich. But that wasn't the only thing Gucci gave me at the shoot. I got to keep the mascara, and then a couple of weeks later I got an email from someone at Gucci who told me I could go to my nearest shop and pick out whatever I wanted. They said I could have anything! Can you imagine? It's like all my dreams – and my daydreams – had come true. I went into London with Mum and Amy to visit the Gucci store. They made me feel so special. It was like I was in a film!

I picked out a sparkly hair clip that said 'Gucci' in big letters and a soft, silky scarf. I also got a lovely dress and some shoes. I felt like I should leave it there – even though I wanted everything – because I didn't like to take too much. They were so kind. They also gave Amy thirty per cent off a pair of shoes she liked.

A little while later, Gucci invited me to do an online event with them. It was towards the end of the pandemic and still very tricky to travel, so I joined them on Zoom. It was hosted by Gian Luca Bauzano, an Italian journalist, and there was a panel of other people. It was on the telly in Italy and featured in the newspapers as well. The whole thing took two hours to record. It took a long time because I don't speak Italian, so we needed a translator to explain what I was saying to them and what they were saying to me.

They asked me to show them around my house, so I carried the laptop into each room and showed them the photos I had in my room and introduced them to our dog. They hadn't warned us that they were going to ask for a tour, so thank goodness the house is always pretty tidy! Before the event, a beautiful package arrived containing two Gucci dresses and a sweatshirt with Mickey Mouse on the front. Then at Christmas they sent another pack with their new collection of nail polishes and new eyeliners and lip liners, too. I loved it all!

The advert was supposed to come out in April, but because of the pandemic they pushed it back to June. While we were waiting for everyone to see the lovely pictures, Zoe from Zebedee called Mum and said, 'You need to be prepared for what's going to happen.' Mum said, 'Why? What's going to happen?' I don't think any of us expected a big fuss. We were very naive… because it all completely kicked off!

When the advert came out, everybody loved it. It turns out I had made history as the first model with Down syndrome to feature in an advert for a high-end fashion brand. It was a really big deal, but I don't think we realised that at the time. I'm not sure if it's sunk in even now! When Gucci posted my picture on their Instagram page it quickly became one of their most-liked posts of all time – it had more than 850,000 likes!

The pictures were everywhere. We were in local newspapers like the *Essex Chronicle* and the *Ilford Recorder*, but also in all the big ones. My story was in the *Daily Mirror*, the *Daily Mail*, *Metro*, *Hello!* magazine and loads of others. They put in pictures of Mum and Dad, too, and some of Amy. Everyone wanted to know about my life, and people said I was 'inspirational' and 'breaking boundaries'. I just thought I was being me! The truth is, my images were continuing an important conversation about diversity, inclusion and representation within the fashion industry, something fashion insider Zadrian Smith told us is vital, given that 'the fashion industry as a whole has not been built to be inclusive'.

He added: 'Minorities, whether that be through size, sexuality, race or disability, haven't been painted into the picture, and we see that reflected in what fashion has to offer, who controls the industry and who it caters towards. However, the high street has started to make big moves in recent years, with many high-street brands catering to a more inclusive size range and representation in all forms in campaigns, for example Kurt Geiger's 'People Empowered' campaign launched in 2020, which continues to spotlight a diverse range of individuals [including Ellie] to raise awareness around important issues such as racism, disability, the climate crisis and much more.

'We need more of this to start making waves, as sadly the luxury industry is still quite far behind in this regard, especially in terms of inclusivity. We are starting to see a more inclusive representation on the catwalks, with designers such as Moschino and Valentino showcasing a representation of size, race and gender on the catwalks, but this often isn't filtering down to representation in the collection sizing.

'I've seen small pockets of hope over the years, such as the rise in diversity initiatives proposed after the impact of BLM [Black Lives Matter], but it never seems to quite stick. It comes down to the fact that, no matter what, the industry knows consumers will continue to buy despite the lack of diversity, inclusivity and representation, which makes it even more imperative that change comes from within the industry itself. Having these tough conversations and holding the industry accountable is the first step, and the only way the fashion and entertainment space will start to make way for important voices from every walk of life.'

Zadrian's comments helped me realise how ground-breaking that Gucci campaign was, but at the time we could barely take it all in! There was so much going on at the time, and Mum's phone was constantly ringing with offers for modelling or requests for interviews. Buzzfeed wrote an article that listed the most important pictures of Alessia Glaviano's career, and my photo was one of them.

In an interview about the photo she said, 'This image is a symbol of my commitment. It went viral, the image and the story, and Ellie is now a model who works a lot. I am so happy about this. If there's one thing I'm very proud of and I want to keep doing, it's work like this.'[1]

A few years ago, there was no way I could have imagined that one of the most important women at *Vogue* would be speaking about my photo in interviews. It just shows that you never know what's around the corner... and there was still more to come for me.

---

1 P. Peterson, 'These Are The Iconic Photographs That Defined A Vogue Editor's Career': https://www.buzzfeednews.com/article/piapeterson/vogue-italia-editor-alessia-glaviano-photos-inspiring (accessed 27 April 2023).

30

Little sister, big dreams

Amy again

The day Mum phoned me to say that Ellie had been signed by a modelling agency was the most excited I've ever been. I couldn't believe there was an agency specifically for models, actors and dancers with additional needs. It was perfect for Ellie. When she first started, about seven years ago, it felt like there was no diversity anywhere. I never saw people with disabilities in fashion campaigns – and rarely on the telly. It does feel like everything's changed since then. There's so much more inclusivity, and Ellie's played an incredible part in that.

Ellie's platform means that she gets loads of messages from people, and they're almost all kind and encouraging. But I do worry because not everyone is nice, especially on the internet. I feel concerned that people won't treat her well, when she's just so enthusiastic and positive about everything. I hate the idea of trolls being rude to her.

When one of Ellie's big campaigns came out, I started seeing her picture everywhere. People were sending it to me from all sorts of different Instagram accounts and from all over the world. Then one night I sat up for hours and read every comment I could find about her. I read through thousands and thousands, poring over every word. It was overwhelmingly positive, with almost everyone praising Ellie and the brand for the ground-breaking photos and saying how beautiful she was. I was shocked. I had assumed there would be more hatred.

But then I found a really nasty one. The commenter was a teenage girl. I would guess that she was fifteen or so, but I couldn't tell. She had written that Ellie couldn't even say the brand name, let alone model for them. I felt hurt and upset reading it. So I did what you're definitely not supposed to do, and I replied. I said that Ellie had obviously done better than her, as Ellie was getting paid to be a model while she was sitting at home writing mean comments. The girl didn't respond after that, which is probably for the best.

I know it's better not to engage with trolls, but I just wanted to defend Ellie. I do feel protective of her, and I want her to feel the same kindness that she puts out into the world. I don't read the comments any more – mainly because I trust that the people who follow Ellie online really do care about her, and they mostly write lovely things, but also because I'm no longer concerned. I've seen Ellie take so much in her stride that I believe she could handle a few thoughtless words if she had to. She doesn't care what other people think of her. I would find it difficult if I knew it upset her, but she's so resilient I have nothing to worry about.

It's not just social media that has brought out my protective side when it comes to Ellie; it's her social life, too. I'm so desperate for her to only spend time with people who see her full value and treat her really well. I want her to have a full life, and that means getting out and about, and meeting and dating people. I know Ellie wants to go out on a Saturday night like her friends from dance class, and she doesn't want me or Mum or Dad to be with her, but that's just not possible. It's really hard for us all to find a balance between what's most fun for her and what's safest.

Of all the challenges I have experienced from having a sister with Down syndrome, helping my parents navigate that has been the toughest. There are so many different levels of Down's, and no two people are the same. There are people who are virtually able to function like anybody else and those whose lives are severely affected. With Ellie, she's quick and with it. She knows what she wants, but she's also vulnerable and needs extra care. I totally understand why she wants to be out all the time. When I was twenty-one my parents hardly saw me – I was constantly out at clubs and seeing my friends. But sadly, it can't be the same for Ellie.

Aside from that, there's so much I love about having her as a sister. She's hilarious. Honestly, laugh-out-loud funny. She can be a handful, and obviously we're sisters so we've argued plenty of times, but I do think she has the best sense of humour of anyone I know. Her comic timing is so on point – she comes out with the perfect funny comments.

She's also very open, and she reminds me of Grandma Freda in that way. Ellie welcomes everyone with open arms. She's so loving, but also never afraid to say what she's thinking, which can have me hiding in embarrassment sometimes. But she doesn't mind. She's just completely herself.

I couldn't be prouder of Ellie. Every time a new and incredible job comes in, I feel shocked all over again. I can't believe people actually know who she is, and that if you google her she's everywhere! When I think about how well she's done, and is still doing, it feels like it's not real. Sometimes I go with her on shoots, and I can't believe how professional she is. She can be acting like a total nutter around the house, but when she gets on set and she's working, it's like she's a totally different person. It's hard work for anyone, let alone someone with a disability, but she takes it all in her stride. She is completely unfazed by anything, and I don't think she even realises how remarkable she is.

31

Working nine to five

Ellie again...

Things changed after the Gucci campaign. I started getting messages from people I'd been at school with, and some people I hadn't spoken to for ages were saying we were friends. A lot of the messages were lovely, and it was really nice to know that people were supporting me and cheering me on. But sometimes it felt like people were jealous. Some made comments about how surprised they were that I'd been a success or that I could be a model. I just ignored them. There were lots of people saying nice things, too, and that's all that really mattered to me.

More and more offers came in, and lots of them didn't even ask me to do castings any more. I felt like a famous model! I got a call from *YOU* magazine, who wanted me to do a photo shoot for their fashion issue. They asked me and Mum about my life and all the difficulties when I was born. Mum watched while I did the photo shoot. I wore loads of different outfits, some clothes from Topshop and H&M, and some designer ones, too. They put me in a really sparkly dress from RIXO, which was covered in sequins. Then I wore a bright-red dress from Valentino with a white collar, and cuffs with lace on. My very favourite was a brown maxi dress by Samantha Sung. It had long sleeves and the material was floaty, all the way down to the floor. I swooshed it up for the pictures, so it looked like I'd been caught in the wind. It was a long day, but a lot of fun.

The next magazine that asked me to appear for them was *Glamour*, but this time they wanted me on the cover! We did the whole shoot in summer because I was going to be on the front of their September issue. That's the biggest issue for fashion magazines.

Zebedee called to give us the good news, and it just felt like all these amazing things were happening at once. It was a real 'wow' moment – and of course I did some screaming to celebrate! I spoke to their journalist Josh Smith, who asked me all about myself. I told him I wanted to represent all people with disabilities… and that I wanted to show myself off to the world.

This time they went full glam with my styling. I guess that makes sense, as it's called *Glamour* magazine! They poofed up my hair, so it had lots of volume, and put bright-red lipstick on my lips. There were a lot of costume changes, and the theme of the shoot was 'gold'. I wore a yellow Gucci dress and a lovely gold jacket. That's the one that ended up in the cover shot. They also put a big chunky cuff at the top of my ear to match the theme. It pinched a lot, but it looked great in the photos. In some of the other shots they put gold leaf on the inside of my eyes, and they used some as eyeshadow. They tied my hair into a low ponytail with a centre parting, then put a row of gold leaf along the middle. It looked so different – like nothing I'd ever done before. Then for the final shot they pulled my hair back away from my face, like when you've just come out of the bath, and added gold leaf all over my head. It went all through my hair – it was a nightmare to get out again.

They arranged for Cartier to lend them some jewellery for the shoot, but Cartier stuff is so expensive that they sent two bodyguards to watch over it! They were standing at the back of the room on guard the whole time. It was like I was wearing the crown jewels. When we were finished taking pictures I started taking everything off, but I couldn't undo the bracelet. I pulled at it to see if it would come off, but they ran across the room to stop me and take it off themselves!

I've done seven magazine covers now, but that first one was special. I remember the day a big brown envelope arrived on the mat. It was a printed copy of my *Glamour* cover. Pulling it out of the envelope and seeing my face was just magical. I ran around the house waving it. I was just so excited to show Amy and my dance teacher Beca.

I did another cover shoot for *Allure* magazine straight after that. This one was different; it was very arty and the pictures were a bit more serious. But the interview was as fun and cheeky as normal – just how I like it! Then Primark asked me to model some of their clothes for a set of massive posters that went up in their flagship store on Oxford Street.

There were lots more shoots towards the end of 2020, like the Sports Direct TV advert and photos for the Avon catalogue. I also modelled clothes for Amazon and Zalando, and Kurt Geiger asked me to model shoes for them. They still send me the most incredible heels in the post every now and again!

I started to get used to modelling, and I loved every second of it. A lot of people have asked if I find it difficult to be a model or a dancer, but the answer is always no. I'm doing what I love to do and it doesn't feel like hard work at all. At every photo shoot everyone has treated me with a lot of respect and been very kind, and I try to do the same. Sometimes if it's a really long day I need breaks, but I'm sure you're like that at your job too, right? If I get tired, I usually have a snack and then I'm back to normal and ready to go.

I get paid for all my modelling jobs – but I'm not telling you how much! I joked to Mum that I'm saving up for a Lamborghini, but I'm not really. I don't drive.[1] I don't feel like doing all these modelling jobs has really changed me. I love showing the world who I am and what I'm capable of, but at the end of the day I'm still the same Ellie, and nothing fazes me.

---

1 Yvonne: Except driving me and your dad up the wall!

32
Flying high

If there is one thing that can make me feel a bit too big for my boots, it's when a brand flies me to another country for a photoshoot. That feels fabulous, and it's happened a few times now, but it's not always as glamourous as people think. Mostly it's very busy, so there isn't a lot of time for sightseeing.

Mum and I have flown to Italy, Sweden and Germany for different jobs. We loved them all, but Germany was my favourite. We went to Hamburg to shoot for a luxury fashion website called Mytheresa. They met us off the plane and took us to a five-star hotel, and we each got a massive bed to ourselves. For the shoot I had to dance all day to music from a live brass band – it was so much fun!

Milan was a great shoot, too. They gave me a burger and chips for dinner (I ate it all!), and we had a whole afternoon to walk around and see the sights. But it was in June, so it was way too hot for me – we were melting!

Sweden was a tricky one. It was for a clothing brand called Kappahl. I got the job during the pandemic, so travelling was very difficult. We were allowed to go abroad for work, but there weren't many flights then because people weren't moving between countries much. We had to fly to Paris to get a plane to Sweden, but it was a bit of a palaver, and in the end our flight from Paris was cancelled. We had to stay in a tiny hotel by the airport that night. We got to Stockholm eventually, but we missed the first day of the shoot!

The pandemic also meant we had to turn down a lot of other jobs. The only one I'm really sad about is for Rihanna's brand Fenty. I would have loved to model for Fenty, but the shoot was in America and that just wasn't possible during Covid.

The jobs kept coming and I built up an amazing portfolio. In the first half of 2021 I was on the cover of *Elle*'s American–Mexican edition, and of *Mission* and *Euphoria.* magazines. I did an editorial spread for *Elle Serbia*, which was a really fun shoot. We took the pictures in London, and they blasted out Christmas songs and took photos while I sang away to Mariah Carey and George Michael. Then all the electricity went off, so they were running around trying to sort that out. I quite enjoyed the chaos of it – especially as I loved the team working on the shoot.

Then *Vogue* asked me to be on their YouTube channel, which is so iconic! I couldn't believe it when they said they wanted me to record my skincare routine. We decided to film it at Amy's flat, as she had more space in her bathroom. Vogue sent over all the equipment we needed from America, but as the pandemic was still ongoing, we had to set it up ourselves. We had a special tripod, and lighting and recording equipment. It was all so professional. They talked Mum through setting it all up, but she still got a little flustered!

I had my skincare products ready, and once we were rolling we just had to keep going without stopping the tape. So if I made a mistake, I had to redo that part and they would edit out the recorded bits they didn't need. It was lucky they could edit it, because at one point I picked up a face mist spray and didn't check the direction the nozzle was facing. I sprayed it straight into my eye! Mum rushed me to the sink and I had to rinse it out, all while the camera was still rolling. We managed to get it out but my eye was a bit red, and you can still see that in some of the end shots of the video.

I was getting more and more commercial photo shoots, and I did a big campaign for TK Maxx. They had me try on loads of different outfits and dance around wearing them, so I was in my element. Even though that was a few years ago now, I still sometimes see those pictures on big posters inside the store and in the shop windows.

I also modelled some of Victoria's Secret's PINK activewear – not the lacy underwear, thank you very much! We did loads of shots at an East London studio, and then they had a car take us out and about. We took photos at Columbia Road Flower Market, on Brick Lane and on a basketball court. It was a twelve-hour day, but they gave me ice cream, so I managed to keep my energy levels up. At the end of the shoot I got to take home the basketball and nine amazing hoodies – I still wear them all the time.

It was in June 2021 that I signed my first year-long contract as a model and brand ambassador for Adidas. They had so many amazing plans for how we could work together, and it was an incredible next step for my career. We started with the campaign for their new sports bra in the September. It was called 'Support Is Everything', and it was a chance to do my favourite thing (dance) with one of my favourite people (my dance teacher Beca)!

They told me I could have someone else there doing the dancing with me, so I chose her straight away. Beca is always so encouraging, and she's taught me so much. I knew I wanted her to come and dance in the advert. It was a really long day – we were filming for a whole twelve hours, even though the advert was less than a minute long – but it's always like that. Their photographer, Sophie Ebrard, also took a lot of pictures of me that day. One of them ended up winning the Taylor Wessing Photographic Portrait Prize in 2022, so once again I was on display at the National Portrait Gallery.

Beca's view

I couldn't believe it when Yvonne called me to tell me the news. First that Ellie was going to be in such an incredible and high-profile campaign, and second that she needed a supporting dancer, and she'd picked me. I asked Ellie if she was sure – didn't she want her mum or her sister? But she was certain she wanted to dance with me. That's the thing with Ellie, she's so kind and loyal. I'm not the only one who teaches Ellie at Straight Up Dance and Theatre School. We have loads of other instructors, even people from the

Pussycat Dolls, dance troop Flawless and big dance films. But she's always said I'm her favourite because I'm the one who gave her a chance. She came to me because she didn't want to be held back and needed an extra push, so we've always done that. To be asked to dance with her after seeing how far she's come was an honour.

Of course, I agreed straight away and we did some prep beforehand. We came up with three routines in advance so that the Adidas team would have a lot of options to choose from. On the day we did our choreography but we freestyled a lot. We just mucked around and had fun with it. I couldn't believe how professional Ellie was once the cameras started rolling. They worked her hard, but she kept going and made sure she delivered the shots they needed.

They were so attentive to Ellie, and it was the first time I realised what a big deal she is! Nothing was too much trouble. They offered her drinks, a sit-down, a bite to eat – anything she could ask for – but she took it all in her stride.

On a personal level, I felt like the campaign was just what I needed. I was a professional dancer for years, having trained at the prestigious performing arts school Italia Conti in London. I auditioned all the time, but got so sick of people telling me yes or no based on one small thing about my looks or my training, so I started going down the choreography route. In the end I opened the school to show people that everyone is good enough to dance and everyone is welcome. We need people like Ellie to show us how to handle life's speed bumps and pivots.

As a teacher, you assume you've hung up your dancing shoes. And although you can't tell, I was eight weeks pregnant when we filmed that shoot. I felt sick the whole time, but pushed through. I was worried about wearing the crop top and leggings, but quickly realised that was what it was all about; showing off all shapes and sizes. So I had to get over any body hang-ups and embrace it!

The experience confirmed for me that I want to keep dancing until I physically can't any more, and I want to give others the chance to do the same. I'm so proud of what we both achieved that day. And I was even prouder when I started seeing the pictures on billboards on the tube and when a friend sent me a picture of the advert in France. The real cherry on top was when the advert was up in Times Square in New York and ran during the Super Bowl. If you'd have told me I'd be dancing in front of such a huge audience one day, I never would have believed you!

Back to Ellie

In October I did a photoshoot for Adidas's 'Always Original' campaign. There was a bit of filming, too, and I wore some of my favourite Adidas clothes: a bright green T-shirt and a cosy orange jumper. After that we filmed the 'Impossible Is Nothing' commercial. I danced down a train and posed in the aisle. It was a lot of fun. When they made the advert they used videos from some of the other shoots I'd done with them. I recorded a voice-over, and I remember it ending with: 'I was born this way – fierce! My story is not impossible because *I'm* possible!' I loved the empowering message.

At the beginning of 2022, Adidas called me again because they were doing a fun project where they were putting statues of inspirational women up in London. They said they had found out there were more statues of animals than women in the capital and they wanted to put that right. They wanted me to be one of their statues. A *statue*! I had already been in a Christmas advert, appeared in *Vogue* and modelled for Gucci, and now they were making a statue of me! It was just unbelievable. There were eight of us altogether: me; Arsenal footballer Vivianne Miedema; footballer and commentator Eniola Aluko; footballer and CEO of Goals4Girls Francesca Brown; rugby player Emily Scarratt; youth worker and activist Tanya Compas; basketballer and activist Asma Elbadawi; and dancer and UN advocate Sherrie Silver. What incredible women!

I had to go in and have a full body scan so they could make a mould to create my statue. I stood nice and tall, with one hand on my hip and the other high in the air. When the statue was finished, they painted it blue and put it on a red plinth by the river in

London with the other seven. It was the coolest thing ever seeing a statue of myself. I was so proud.

Just when I thought things couldn't get any better, they asked me to design my own Adidas dress – just like all the celebrities. I made my dress pale lilac with big white writing on the back saying 'role model'. Down one arm it said 'Ellie', because I *am* a role model! I love it, and I gave one to each of the girls at my dance class: Lily, Joy, Katie and my teacher Beca. I also got to design my own trainers with the Adidas teams in Singapore and the US. These were based on the Ozweego-style trainer, and are pink and beige with leopard-print sections.

The work with Adidas felt important because it was all about showing what different people can do, as well as supporting one another and believing in yourself. I liked the fact that even though it was my work, it had an important message.

I've done some work with charities, too. I contributed to a CoppaFeel! campaign to help people get to know their bodies and recognise the signs of cancer. Then Mencap asked me to take part in their myth-busters campaign. My myth-busting statement was: 'People with a learning disability can't be successful fashion models… just look at me'.

More campaigns continued to come through, such as Laura Mercier, Space NK and Primark Beauty. I also did a great *Marie Claire* magazine shoot. I did lots of TV interviews and got to meet so many famous people. I spoke to Michael Ball on Zoom, and he was so nice. He put on one of my favourite songs – 'Perfect' by Ed Sheeran – and danced with me on the screen! I went on *Loose Women* via Zoom, too. I was supposed to go to the studio, but it all got changed at the last minute.

That's when I met Katie Piper for the first time. I loved her straight away; she was so warm. Mum bought her book *Beautiful* after that. She read it, and I read some bits with her. As I bet you already know, Katie is such an inspiring woman.

Other than Katie Piper, my favourite celebrity I met was Kate Garraway. She told me she thought I would get on the cover of *Vogue*! I met her and Adil Ray when I went on *Good Morning*

Britain to talk about being the cover star for *Fabulous* magazine and also for winning its Woman of the Year gong. I had to sit far away from them because Covid rules still applied. They called me a 'trailblazing top model' and I talked to them about how a wider variety of people should be represented in the fashion and beauty industry. I flicked my hair a lot and they loved it.

One thing they asked was who inspired me, and that gave me an opportunity to say thank you to my mum. You've read all the way to this point, so you know how much she loves and looks after me, but it was special to get the opportunity to say it to the nation on telly. When Adil asked me who I looked up to when I was growing up, I said, 'I think my mum, because she is so nice, and she supports me with everything that I do. She takes me to college, she takes me into my shoots, she gets me there on time.' Of course, I mentioned my sister Amy and my dad, too!

For the rest of the year I modelled for lots of other brands: Body Shop, Boots, Spotify and Barbie. But my favourite shoot of all time was for George at Asda. It wasn't the biggest or the fanciest, but it was a lot of fun. I think it might have been a bit more fun because Mum wasn't there watching me! She couldn't come that day, so she sent one of her friends to look out for me instead. The job was for Asda's 'Fenomenal' femininity campaign, and there were lots of other great women modelling for them. I did an interview with Asda where they asked me what femininity meant to me, I said it was about being strong. We took pictures of me modelling their clothes and filmed some videos. I was wearing a lovely pink gingham dress with a ruffle at the top. They put curls in my hair – which I loved because it's usually straight – and they gave me a nice pink lip gloss.

When the new campaign came out, Asda invited me to a launch party to celebrate. They had lots of people there and great music. I had a summer mocktail and got a book signed by Bryony Gordon. I loved going to this glam event, as it was one of my first glitzy parties, but I didn't realise then that there would be lots more to come.

33
Winning awards

Everything that was happening felt like it was a dream instead of my actual life. It was hard to get my head around the amazing opportunities I was given, especially when some people had said I wouldn't be able to achieve anything. Just when I thought there was no way things could any get better, *Glamour* magazine told me they were giving me their Gamechanging Model award.

They sent a whole crew to my house to present me with the award, which was unusual as many large events were still happening remotely. This included a make-up artist, a hairdresser, a stylist, a photographer, a videographer and loads of other people. They spent a couple of hours getting me all dressed and ready, and then we went to a park to film my acceptance speech. It was twenty minutes away, but they wanted a pretty outdoor setting for the short film. The only problem was, it was January – and I was freezing!

All I remember is how cold I felt. They put me in a lovely dress and a red cape with no sleeves. I'm sure my arms went purple because it was so chilly. I was wearing a pair of Gucci shoes, but they got muddy walking through the park. They brought lots of water bottles and a massive quilt for me to cuddle up in when I wasn't filming. I recorded the message accepting the award and held it up high. I think I was shaking the whole time, but they said I did well. In my speech, I said: 'Thank you, *Glamour*, for my award. I love you so much. Bye!'

Later that year I heard from *Fabulous* magazine that I had won another award, as I was one of their ten Women of the Year. Other women on the list included Alison Hammond, Adele and the Queen! I couldn't believe I was in there with them. It didn't feel real. We did a fun pink photoshoot in an East London studio, and I wore lots of different clothes. Then they put my photo on the cover of the magazine! I was wearing a big fluffy cream dress with black polka dots and ankle boots. They did some filming with me, too, where I answered questions about modelling and my family, and how I like to inspire other people.

Once parties were back in full swing, I met Judge Rinder at a Method cleaning products party and taught him how to pose like a model. Some of the people from *Married at First Sight* were there, so I had a dance with them later in the night. I was also invited to an amazing event at the big Lego store in central London with a red carpet and celebrity guests. They gave me loads of Lego sets and even made an Ellie Lego person that I got to take home with me as a gift, along with a Lego Harry Potter keyring that I gave to Amy.

My favourite party was the 2022 *Glamour* awards. It was the first one they had held in five years because of all the lockdowns, and I was invited! My mum got me ready. She did my hair and make-up, and I wore a pretty blue dress that London-based designer brand Sister Jane had sent me. I felt like a star – especially when I got out of the car and walked along the red carpet. There were loads of photographers standing behind a metal barrier taking my picture, and the lights were flashing constantly. I did my best poses and flicked my hair. It was like something I usually would have watched on TV.

Once we got inside, Mum found our table and we were sitting with the celebrities – like we were one of them! I met Rita Ora and had a picture with her, and Dermot O'Leary, too. But my favourite was the singer Anne-Marie. I love dancing to her music, so I couldn't believe it when I saw she was there. I went over to her straight away and asked for a picture. Mum took it for me, and it was the best photo of the whole night.

A word from Yvonne

I couldn't believe all this was happening. From the parties and the statue to the magazine covers and Gucci, it's been a whirlwind. Just when something amazing happened and I thought, *Nothing can top that*, another job came along that did! It isn't always easy, though, and Ellie's work involves long days. People often confirm photo shoots at the last minute, and there can be a flurry of two or three jobs in one week and then nothing the next.

After Ellie's work kicked off, I gave up my part-time job as a support worker for young adults with special needs. At first I tried to do both, but it wasn't sustainable. I kept having to ask for time off to take Ellie to auditions or to go on shoots. When the pandemic happened, it felt like the natural time to take a step back. With Ellie home all the time, I couldn't go into work anyway. But even when the lockdown rules eased up, I decided it wouldn't work for me to go back. I travel with Ellie everywhere and sit in on a lot of her shoots. Other times I'll wait outside until she's done. The days are often long, and it is quite tiring. I miss doing my own work, but it's just turned out this way. We can't all have everything. I've had to make sacrifices for my kids, and I'm OK with that. I love Ellie, and I could never let her miss out on these once-in-a-lifetime opportunities.

On the whole, we don't spend too much time thinking about the rollercoaster ride we've been on with Ellie's work. We're just us; our family at home in Essex watching *I'm a Celeb* and deciding what to have for tea. But then sometimes it hits me out of the blue, and I'll look up at Mark and say, 'It's unbelievable what's going on, isn't it?' And sometimes he'll say the same to me. We have to just laugh… there's nothing else we can do!

It's weird that people recognise Ellie now, and that if you google her name she's everywhere. I feel so proud. I'm proud of her strength and her courage and her heart. I love that she chats to everyone and is so warm and welcoming. And I love that the world can see Ellie's achievements and realise that everyone is capable of so much more than some people might think.

34

Auntie Ellie

Ellie continues

There wasn't just great stuff happening with my work during this time; our family was growing, too. In spring 2021, Amy and her partner Richie invited me for a hot chocolate at Costa. I ordered a chocolate Frostino and a chocolate wafer from the counter (my favourites at the time!), and once we had our drinks we found a table and sat down.

It was then that they told me they were expecting a baby and I was going to be an auntie. I screamed in the middle of the coffee shop, and everyone turned around to look at me. I jumped up and gave them a massive hug and said, 'Congratulations!' They hadn't told me straight away. They'd waited until it was past twelve weeks because they knew I'd be so excited that I'd tell everybody!

That August, Amy had a joint baby shower with her friend who was due four weeks after her. It was a lot of fun. There were so many people there, and loads of food and drinks. They had a big cake and a wall of doughnuts. They asked a party designer to make them a massive hoop covered in green, cream and brown balloons with dried flowers and leaves, like pampas grass and ferns. It looked magical, and I took loads of pictures with Mum and Amy standing in front of it. I wore a brown dress and two clips in my hair. Amy looked beautiful in a pink dress that came off her shoulders, and with her hair long and wavy.

Everyone turned up with presents for the baby. I brought a Moses basket made of wicker for him or her to sleep in once the baby was born. Amy didn't find out the sex before the birth, but she knew it was going to be a girl. She could just tell. We couldn't wait to welcome her into the family.

On 6 September I was having a bath in the evening when I heard a massive noise. Mum was screaming and the dog was barking, and I couldn't work out what was going on. I got out of the bath and wrapped a towel around myself, then opened the door and shouted to Mum, 'What's going on?' She just shouted back, 'I have a grandson! I have a grandson!' She was shouting at Dad, too. She was very loud!

I was so happy for Amy and Richie, but also surprised that they had a boy because Amy had been so sure it was a girl. She had even bought girls' clothes! They had picked out the name Mia, but of course they couldn't use that any more. So instead, they called him Blake. It was a perfectly healthy delivery and Amy was doing well. She just needed to stay in hospital overnight to rest and start her recovery. We weren't allowed to go in and see her, as the hospital was strict about visitors, so we had to wait to meet him.

Amy and Richie came over the next day and brought Blake to meet us all. It was the first time I had met a baby, so I was very emotional. He was so small, and his face was all scrunched up, but he looked healthy, not weird. He was clean and a normal colour. He was wearing a white Babygro that was a bit too big for him, and he looked like a doll. I thought he was very cute. I cried; it was such a special moment. I was looking at him, and Amy asked me, 'Do you love him?' I started crying again and said, 'Yes. I love him!'

Now we have a baby around all the time. Amy doesn't live far away, so she comes over with Blake a lot. Mum helps look after him sometimes and I get to play with him. I'm going to be his cool auntie, and I know we're going to have so much fun together when he gets older. I want to sign him up for dance classes straight away, but Amy says he's not coming dancing with me – not yet, anyway! I'm going to get him a mini hula hoop to match the one I have, and I'll take him on the slide and the swings, and teach him how to do a cartwheel.

When he's older I want him to be a singer and a dancer (and a twerker, too!). I want him to work hard at school and get good grades, but for his job I want him to perform on stage like Boy George or Harry Styles. That said, I want him to feel like he can be anybody he wants to be. I've always been just Ellie, and he should get a chance to be just Blake.

35
Influencing

Social media is good and bad all at the same time. I don't spend a lot of time on there, and Mum helps me with my Instagram. I started getting a lot of followers when I did the modelling jobs, and now I've got thousands and thousands. A lot of people want to know about my life, and it's nice to feel like I have lots of support.

Sometimes social media can be very stressful, but I think everyone finds that, don't they? I don't read through the comments, but Mum has a look sometimes and people usually say really nice things. Although occasionally it's not like that and people can be nasty.

When I was just getting started with my career and Instagram gave me a blue tick so that people would know it was definitely me on my page, my account was hacked. We opened up Instagram on Mum's phone to post something and suddenly realised we couldn't log in. We were locked out, and couldn't access the account with the usual username and password. It was weird because the profile picture had changed, too, and we hadn't done that. Whoever was in my profile had deleted all my pictures. It felt really scary. We didn't know how they had got in or what else they could log in to.

Amy was furious and got her phone out straight away. She sent a message to the hackers via my account, telling them it was her sister's account. They actually replied and told her to leave them alone or they would hack her account as well. But she said, 'No! You get off, or I'll report you.'

We reported it to Instagram, but as we didn't get an instant reply we decided it was best to report it to the police, and we told them everything that had happened. We were worried that the nasty people who had stolen my account would post a bad picture to all my followers and we wouldn't be able to stop them. The hackers started sending messages to my followers saying horrible things. They messaged one of my friends asking for naked pictures and they sent lots of people strange memes. Thankfully, most people could tell it wasn't me, but we had to send out lots of messages explaining that my account had been hacked. It was a nightmare.

Amy managed to get back into my profile and quickly changed all the passwords to lock the hackers out. I don't know how she did it, but she's really good with computers. I was so pleased to have it all back. Losing control of my own page made me feel very strange and vulnerable; like someone had broken into my house and was going through the drawers in my bedroom.

Even though we went through all of that, social media is absolutely positive for me. I love TikTok and Instagram, and all the wonderful comments people leave to say hi to me. My followers are very kind and complementary, especially about my eyelashes and eyebrows. I get lots of comments saying they're 'on fleek' (stylish). I've met lots of different people in the modelling and disabled communities through social media, and it's great to be connected to them, but it's not the same for everyone. I know lots of people who get horrible messages about the work they do from strangers online.

Norah Myers told us that she sees some people disliking her as just something that comes with her big platform. She said she's realised her work is so much bigger than the few nasty messages she gets, and it allows her to serve all kinds of different communities that don't feel seen in the wellness space – from LGBTQI+ and disabled clients to POC clients and those with chronic conditions like Crohn's and lupus. She said that she gets lots of lovely messages from people in the LGBTQI+ and disabled communities, thanking her for helping them to be more themselves in that area.

I get a lot of direct messages from people who have a family member with Down syndrome. Sometimes they'll send me a photo. The messages are always emotional and moving. They say that I have helped and encouraged them. Some even say their kids want to be like me when they're older! Some parents message and ask for advice on different things for their children with Down syndrome, and Mum messages them back when she has the time. It makes me feel happy to know that there are parents of children with Down's, or people with Down's themselves, who look up to and are inspired by me. I think we all need a role model. We all need to see people who look like us in magazines and on television. I never really saw that when I was growing up, so I love that I can do it for other people.

Yvonne's perspective

I think Ellie is really good with her social media. She knows what sort of stuff to post and will always check a picture with me before she puts it online. We do it together, but she's the one who shows me how to use all the features – like tagging people. She picks it all up very quickly and is way better than me, but I guess all parents feel that way about their children and technology!

Instagram is very time-consuming. It takes a while to choose the pictures or videos and get them ready to post. It can feel like a lot of pressure to keep up and find exciting things to share. Sometimes we've done shoots that haven't come out yet, so we're not allowed to post them, and other times Ellie just hasn't done a shoot that week, so we don't have anything for her Instagram. We try not to just fill the gaps with rubbish, but wait until we've got something really fun to upload. I like to read the encouraging comments and will always tell Ellie when someone's written something special. Of course, it's the internet, so it's not all kindness and roses. Some people write nasty things, but I just ignore them. I don't need to tell Ellie about it – she knows people can be horrible sometimes – and I don't want to dwell on that. Sometimes when a magazine or a big designer posts a picture of Ellie it can get up to 4,000 comments. I do my best to read them all, but often there isn't enough time in the day!

I check Ellie's phone every now and again at night to make sure there's nothing on there that shouldn't be, but it's always fine. It doesn't worry me that Ellie has so many followers and such a big online presence, because so much of the response is positive. Maybe if that wasn't the case I would want to stop the social media, but we're part of an encouraging community, and that's how it should be.

36

Ellie's keys to happiness

Back to Ellie

I try not to let things get on top of me and I like to take every-thing in my stride, otherwise things can get me down and it's easy to feel low. We spoke to Dr Julie about staying positive, and she told us that being optimistic is very powerful. It can make you feel less stressed and more motivated. She said that even in our toughest moments, optimism helps us to recognise that those feelings won't last forever and that better times lie ahead. It's especially important when the future is unknown and you can't predict what's coming next, because it helps you to face that future as an adventure and find meaning along the way.

Even when I do my best, though, I sometimes still feel sad. No one is happy all the time, are they? There are some things that make me feel better when I'm feeling sad, and I want to share them with you in case they're helpful for you on a down day.

1 **Dancing with videos**
My secret confession is that I love to watch dance videos on YouTube… especially my own! I like to watch them and try to dance along to see if I remember the moves. It's not just my videos that I like dancing to, though. I like the street dance classes or just music videos where I can copy the singers as they perform. It always makes me feel more upbeat.

2 **Singing in the shower or in your room**
When I sing, I like to sing loudly. That's why the shower is

good, because the noise of the water means people can't hear me so well. You can sing in your room – or anywhere, really.

3 Calming down
Sometimes I feel really stressed or frustrated, and when I'm in that mood I never react very well. The best thing I can do is try to calm down. I take a really deep breath and try to relax as much as possible.

4 Talking to someone
I haven't always been great at sharing my emotions, but I've learnt that I always feel better once I've shared how I'm feeling with someone else. I have my mum and my dad to talk to, and I speak to Amy, too. It doesn't always have to be family, though. I love talking to Beca. She's very kind and understanding.

5 Playing with a hula hoop
I love my hula hoop! It was £30 from Etsy and it's so much fun. You need a bit of space in your house, otherwise you'll knock things over. Maybe you don't like the idea of a hula hoop. If not, there are lots of other things that are simple but will help you move about. What about skipping? Or going for a run? I don't like running, but I know a lot of other people do.

6 Holding hands with a friend
It's really comforting to hold hands with someone, because it means they're there for you when you're sad. And you know that's true because they're physically showing you.

7 Taking your mind off it
Sometimes if I feel sad I like to go and do something happy, or I play an upbeat song or watch a positive film. It helps me to concentrate on something other than the problem. It doesn't always work, but sometimes it means I have time to think, and that's always helpful.

8 Living life to the full

It's always sad if you think you're missing out on fun, but you don't need to wait to be invited. Make your own fun! You can join a dance or drama club like me and meet new people. Or you can start chasing a dream you thought you could never achieve – like me and the modelling! Whatever you want to do, make sure you give it a try. And enjoy it, too!

37
The future

So much has happened already that I don't even know what to expect in the future. I never imagined any of this would happen in the first place! I'm so proud that I have now written a book. I'm proud that people will get to know a bit more of my story, and will hopefully feel encouraged to chase their own dreams.

At home, I would like to keep working towards a bit more independence. I love hanging around with Mum, Dad and Amy, but all my friends from dance class go out and about, and I would like to have just a bit more freedom. It's difficult, because I know I have to be safe and stay with the people who care for me, but I also want to be a normal twenty-one-year-old woman.

I wouldn't ever want to live completely on my own. I'll always need to be with family or have someone around to care for me and help me out. I'm not very good at cooking for myself, so I would need to learn more about that. But I did make blackcurrant jellies and cake in lockdown and they were really yummy, so that's a good start. Mum always says I need to get better at the little stuff like keeping my bedroom arranged and turning lights off when I leave a room – but I'm getting there! For now, I'll definitely stay with Mum and Dad. Spending time with them is fun, and I love my room at home.

I'm going to keep dating – I enjoy going on dates. One day I would really like to meet someone special and get married. I'll wear a big white dress and do a special dance at my wedding. Blake will wear a little suit and be my page boy.

At work, I want to keep doing more of what I love – dancing and modelling. I'd love to go over to America and work there. I want to dance and model in more magazines and on TV, too. My ultimate dream was to be on the cover of *Vogue* in a beautiful dress – and on 3 March 2023 I was invited to shoot for British *Vogue* to appear on the cover of the May issue! I literally couldn't believe it. This was so exciting and a real honour. The shoot day was fabulous; I was treated like a queen. The glam team was amazing and two of my dresses were by Gucci. One dress I also got to wear was made-to-measure by the Princess of Wales's designer Emilia Wickstead. It was a lovely red flowing dress. It was a long day, but a totally amazing experience. It was launched on British *Vogue*'s Instagram page on 20 April. I was at college at the time, so my drama teachers let me go online to take a look. I started screaming with shock and excitement, and then I couldn't help but cry. I felt so emotional, it was ridiculous.

I was also chosen by Barbie to represent the launch of the first ever Barbie doll with Down syndrome. It was such an honour to be chosen to do this and represent the Down syndrome community and Barbie. I had a shoot on 18 April 2023 for a huge launch on 26 April. The shoot was great, and I got to see the doll for the first time. She was beautiful. It was strange to see a doll that looked like me. The photos of me and Barbie were featured in all the major press and also online. I feel so privilege to have been chosen to present a doll that other children with Down syndrome can relate to, and to help other children learn more about Down syndrome. It's so incredible. On the same day, I got to appear on the ITV show *This Morning* to talk about *Vogue* and Barbie. The press and coverage for both has been totally crazy, and I know there is much more to come.

Having received an ICON Award in February 2023 for my 'incredible contribution and service to the fashion industry', I really do feel like the sky is the limit. I hope I will keep being a role model for others and show people who want to get into the fashion industry that anything is possible. I hope that designers and brands will keep being inclusive and inviting different people to model for them. I never saw someone with Down's on telly or in magazines when I was younger, and it makes a difference when you see someone who looks like you. I love that I can do that for young people. I think there's still more work to do, but we're moving in the right direction and that's exciting.

Naomi Graham told us she thinks the world is making good progress when it comes to being kinder to people with disabilities. She believes there has been a big change in the way the world sees and understands additional needs. She still hears shocking stories of families experiencing extreme rejection and facing really tough situations, but she also hears about wonderful and kind things people have done for each other. She said that she has seen plenty of young people who, even in the midst of many challenges, have been able to bring hope and joy to other people because of who they are. I'd like to be able to keep doing that, too.

No matter what I end up doing, I'm going to carry on being myself, following my dreams, twerking it out and drinking hot chocolate at Costa – because those are my favourite things and they're the things that make me *me*, not just my disability.

38
Things I wish everyone knew...

Ellie

I wish everyone knew that you can't look at someone and know everything about them. Actually, you can't assume you know *anything* about them. Instead, speak to that person, listen to them and get to know their character. People will surprise you if you give them the chance!

Yvonne

Doctors, nurses and all the other medical staff in hospitals are truly amazing. I know this book started with quite a difficult story about the support I got from the hospital after Ellie's birth, and I do think that team could have done a lot better, but I'm not angry about it now. We've had a lot of contact with hospitals throughout Ellie's life, and on the whole they have been absolutely wonderful. They are our heroes.

Ellie

We're all able to do so much more than people realise. If someone says you can't do something, ignore it and work out for yourself if you can. People who put you down don't realise what you're capable of.

Yvonne

Speak directly to someone with a disability instead of speaking to the person they're with. Don't assume they can't communicate with you – treat them just as you would anyone else. If you need to adjust how you speak to them, do so afterwards.

Ellie

People will do so much better if you encourage them. In everything I do – college, dance and modelling – it makes me so much more enthusiastic when people cheer for me… and then I do it better! Don't forget to encourage someone today.

Yvonne

Don't say mean things. It sounds simple, but you'd be surprised by some of the comments I've had. If someone's rude about Ellie, as far as I'm concerned that's their problem, not hers. Don't assume you know what any parent's life is like – especially not someone who is raising a child with complex needs. Think very carefully before you decide to chip in, because unless they've asked for it, they probably don't need your feedback!

Ellie

I really am happy most of the time, but people often assume that I never feel low and I'm always in a great mood. I do feel low sometimes, and when sad things happen I still have to process them. I'm just like anyone else, even if I show it a little differently.

Yvonne

Don't make mums feel like an inconvenience. Sometimes when I was walking around with Ellie I would feel as if we were in everyone's way, and I'd get nasty looks when she cried. I know all mums feel that way (I definitely did with Amy sometimes), but it's even worse when your child has a disability. It's important that we're all kind and give the person space to deal with their child without the angry looks.

Ellie

Having Down syndrome or another additional need or significant difference doesn't mean you don't get to live your best life. I do lots of fun things all the time. I hang out with my family and dance and perform. My dreams have come true, and Down syndrome has never held me back. If you have someone in your life with

Down's or another disability, get excited about what they *can* do, not worried about what they *can't!*

Yvonne
I believe that the majority of people see Ellie for what she is: a beautiful, inspirational young woman. I think we need to believe that for ourselves sometimes, too, and ignore the people who don't bring out the best in us. The people who are worth keeping in my and Ellie's lives are the ones who really know us and see our value.

Ellie
Don't let the odds stacked against you determine your future. I had loads of odds stacked against me, but that just means I get to stand here today and say, 'Look what I did… against all odds.'

Acknowledgements

There are so many people to say thank you to in my life that I don't know where to start!

Of course, I want to say thank you to my mum. She always believes in me and helps me to achieve everything I want to. She takes me to shoots and castings and interviews, and she's never let anyone hold me back. My dad, too, for all of his support, love and trips to McDonald's! I also want to say thank you to Amy for doing my hair when we were little and helping me get dressed up and play at being a model. You're the best sister, and now you've brought me the best brother-in-law figure in your partner Richie – not to mention the best nephew, Blake! I want to thank my Uncle Mel and his family, who have been a big part of my life and career. My family as a whole has always been so loving and supportive. I also want to acknowledge my wonderful Uncle Laurence, who sadly passed away in 2017 and is massively missed by the entire family.

My dance teacher Beca is awesome. She always cheers for me and listens to me when I want to talk. I love dancing with her! Also Evette, who spent all that time in school with me, helping me to learn and taking me out and about in town. Plus Michelle and everyone else who helped me at school. A massive thank you to Aly and Lydia for all your support during my five years at college. I wouldn't have achieved top grades without you both.

Thank you to my agents, Zoe and Laura, and every single person at Zebedee. You are the most encouraging people, and it is the greatest honour to work with you. And also Mum's friend Emma, who saw them on *GMB* and said we should speak to them.

Thanks to every single brand that has booked me to work with them. I am so grateful that you have celebrated me and are championing diversity in your adverts – thank you! Especially Gucci and

Adidas, the two most exciting campaigns I got to be a part of. And, of course, all the magazines that interviewed me and journalists who wrote about me and said such kind things. I've had really good experiences of working with lovely people in the national press and I am very grateful.

I want to say thank you to all the medical staff who have helped me, too. I know that things don't always go perfectly, but I think the nurses and doctors who have looked after me when I've been unwell are amazing – especially the people at Great Ormond Street who work with unwell children.

Next I want to say thank you to Katie Piper for being a total inspiration and for asking me to write this book. Thanks for believing that I could – and that people would want to read my story. I am so excited about The UnSeen series, and the other people whose books are coming out soon. Thanks as well to Katie's agents at Fresh Partners and publicists at Belle PR, and to everyone in their teams who have cheered me on.

I'd also like to say thank you to Lauren Windle, my editorial consultant, and to all the people at my publisher, SPCK: Elizabeth Neep, my editor; Mark Read, who designed my fantastic cover, and all the other editors and marketing experts who helped make this book what it is.

And last of all, I want to say thanks to you for buying my book and reading my story. Thank you for following me on Instagram or buying a magazine I was in. I feel like the luckiest girl alive, and that's all thanks to you.

If you enjoyed

Against All Odds

you may want to keep your eyes
peeled for all things

Katie Piper's
THE UNSEEN

To be the first to hear more,
follow **Katie Piper** on Instagram:
@katiepiper_